THE DAYS OF
LONDON
PAST

DAVID MATTHEWS

THE DAYS OF LONDON PAST

First published in Great Britain in 2012 by The Derby Books Publishing Company Limited, 3 The Parker Centre, Derby, DE21 4SZ.

This paperback edition published in Great Britain in 2013 by DB Publishing, an imprint of JMD Media Ltd

ISBN 978-1-78091-056-7

Printed and bound in the UK by Copytech (UK) Ltd Peterborough

CONTENTS

INTRODUCTION

I suppose it was inevitable for a history buff like myself who was born well within the sound of Bow Bells, that London would exert an enduring influence and fascination on my imagination. After leaving school and taking up a career in the Square Mile in my mid-teens, it did not take me long to realise that I was walking in the footsteps of millions of Londoners that had gone before. Walking around the wilderness of alleys and passages, courts and thoroughfares, somehow feeling comfortingly familiar, the feeling of continuity was almost tangible. My school studies had told me that the site of the city of Londinium was established once the Romans' invasion strategy had been decided, in AD 43. Needing to carry their army over to the north bank, the Romans found a suitable area of hard ground in the surrounding marshes in order to bridge the Thames. Discovering the advantage of the Thames being tidal in that area, they found their sea-going ships could gain easy access for import and export. Once the bridge was constructed they decided to build their capital city on the north bank, constructing the very same road layout that is now the foundations of Eastcheap, Gracechurch Street, Lower and Upper Thames Street, Fenchurch Street, and Lombard Street. Was it any wonder that I felt I was surrounded by history as I gazed at the River Thames from London Bridge, against the mediaeval backdrop of the Tower of London? Then in the heart of the city itself there was the magnificent grandeur of Wren's St Paul's Cathedral, and the pivotal Royal Exchange building, where all roads seemed to converge. It was after thinking back to those early perceptions of London when I was at my most impressionable, that I decided to write this mini celebration of London history. I felt that by using some of the great London characters who have enriched London's past like Caxton, Pepys, Johnson and Churchill, it was possible to best illustrate London through the centuries in the following short stories. By applying a combination of the knowledge we have of those people and the times they lived in, a healthy dash of fantasy, plus a vigorous leap of the imagination, I hope to bring those times of London past to life. Contemporary theorists have suggested that linear time is itself a figment of the human imagination, in the following pages I have endeavoured to test the theory.

May 2012

1

LONDON
OCTOBER 1476

The large bustling village of Westminster was bathed in a soft orange glow, as the weak autumn sunshine slowly pierced the watery blue skies. Situated about two miles south west of the walled City of London, the abundant trees that surrounded the area were displaying their full autumnal splendour. The well trodden muddy side road that was King Street, led down from the small fashionable village of Charing into Westminster. The road had been made even more slippery than was usual, by the covering of damp decaying leaves. Looking upwards, the skyline was dominated by the imposing grandeur of Westminster Abbey, which had long been a work in progress since the reign of Henry III some 200 years earlier. Scattered around this magnificent structure was a cluster of smaller buildings that formed the Royal Palace of Westminster. Chief among these buildings was Westminster Hall, which stood 40ft high, and possessed an extraordinary hammer beam roof that had been recently added to the original design. The hall on this day was a bustling hive of activity, as for some time it had become the centre of administration and justice. Parliaments were held there, and so were the great royal feasts, which were a popular recreation on Christmas Day and other special occasions. The monks that existed in the Abbey could be seen energetically going about their daily business, as they were the landlords of most of the Westminster properties, and worked alongside the Royal Palace in governing the manor. The King's government in turn made use of the Abbey premises and employed some of the monks directly as administrators.

This concentration of Government in the fast growing suburb of Westminster had originated from the increasing use of the Abbey as a place of Royal Ceremony – both for the coronations and the burials of English Kings. More pragmatically, the walled City of London to the east, had long been granted the right to collect it's own taxes and appoint their own Sheriff from it's thriving business community. This self governing privilege for Londoners came at a price, and clever Kings like the present Edward IV, knew that it was much more lucrative for the crown to allow the city it's independence. As a ruler of London but not a Governor, the King could negotiate from a distance, mutual benefits for both London's business community, and his own Royal Palace of

Westminster. As a result of this arrangement, the whole economy of Westminster had been shaped by the powerful twin influences of both the church and the Royal Palace.

The area now contained many decent lodging houses, designed to accommodate the many visitors who flocked to the Abbey and the Palace, in addition to the resident government classes, courtiers and monks. To provide services for these officials, it was estimated 400 tradesmen, craftsmen, servants and porters, had been recruited into the manor. The obvious attraction for these providers, was the freedom from city taxes and guild restrictions that came with Westminster's sanctuary status. Though still early, the village was already bustling as the colony of Flemish and German tailors, cobblers, hatters and spectacle makers, opened their doors for custom. While at the same time the numerous cook shops were preparing their hot meat pies, and hastily setting up trestle tables laden with jugs of London ale, generously spiced with pepper to add flavour and body. It was at one of these tables that a dark stocky man in his mid twenties swilled deeply from his jug, and then headed swiftly back to the Abbey precinct. Carefully negotiating his way through the crowds of government officials, he entered a small book shop situated next to the Chapter House section of the Abbey.

The man was of Flemish origin, and he was in the employ of a certain William Caxton. His name was Wynkin De Worde.

About 200 yards north of the shop stood the Almonry Gate – it was adjoined by a large house with a small loft jutting out above the Almonry entrance. An outside wooden staircase led up to the loft, where a carpenter was just completing the fitting of a large oak door with several metal bolts. It was just above this activity that a metal plated sign swung gently in the cool autumn breeze. On closer inspection the sign was decorated with a broad red stripe in the fashion of an heraldic shield, and would come to be known as the Sign of the Red Pale. Looking proudly up at the sign, stood an elderly man dressed in emerald green robes laced with gold braid. This was William Caxton. A wealthy merchant, with the shield being his personal crest. Standing alongside him was a portly man resplendently dressed in a religious gown. This was the head of the Almonry – Prior Arundel – and a week previously he had agreed with Caxton an annual rent of £2 13s 4d for the house next to the gate. This arrangement had suited Caxton perfectly for what he had in mind, and he was soon inhabiting the spacious quarters with his wife Maude and daughter Elizabeth. His cousin Richard Caxton, a monk at the Abbey, had also arranged for him to rent the loft separately. This was in addition to the shop premises near the Abbey Chapter House in the Abbey precinct. As Caxton discussed with the Prior his plans for the house, they were interrupted by two scruffy looking characters asking for money. The Almonry was the centre of charitable donations for the poor and needy, but as a consequence it attracted not only the deserving poor, but a fair proportion of the criminal classes. Attracted by the offer of sanctuary from criminal justice at the Abbey, it was no surprise that fugitives and the shiftless gravitated to the area.

Prior Arundel shrewdly scanned their faces before deciding that they were worthy of his charity, and invited them into the Almonry for food and drink. William Caxton watched them disappear before climbing the steps to inspect the carpenter's work. Caxton was pleased to see that the door was sturdy and strong, for he planned for the loft to be a store room, housing the precious commodity that was to be central to his future. Stepping into the loft, the room measured approximately eighteen feet by seven, perfectly adequate for it's planned function. After paying the carpenter, Caxton bolted the door and descended the staircase.

Meanwhile in the small shop in the precinct, Wynkin De Worde was industriously filing and stacking heaps of news sheets, pamphlets, service books and hymn sheets, while all the time supervising the carpenters constructing extra shelves. Excited by both the activity and the new project, at that moment he had no regrets about the decision to leave his adopted town of Bruges in the lowlands of Northern Europe. He had thought long and hard before deciding to travel back to England with his master William Caxton, but the challenge and excitement of beginning a new business venture in Westminster had proved irresistible. The crossing of the channel had not been an easy one. The transportation of their precious cargo had been fraught with difficulty. Still, they had finally arrived safely with everything intact, and he was now ready to put to good use all he had learnt previously in a little room over the porch of St Donat's in Bruges. It had been in that small shop under the supervision of William Caxton and Bruges' native Colard Mansion, that Wynkin had felt that he was at the forefront of something innovative and immensely profitable.

Working alongside Wynkin in the Westminster shop was a young Frenchman from Normandy – his name was Richard Pynson. He was as equally enthused by the venture as Wynkin, and had needed little encouragement to travel to England for their joint enterprise. He was also making himself busy in the shop, categorizing the stacked literature by subject matter and language. In common with their master Caxton, both young men shared a passion for the written word and possessed a voracious appetite for reading and writing. It was this shared enthusiasm that had brought them all together, and now there was a real possibility that for these two young men, it could lead to considerable wealth.

The house that William Caxton had rented was large and extensive. It possessed a spacious area at street level that he had already converted into a shop, with a dividing wall segregating and obscuring a workshop. On the two floors above there was a large dining room, a parlour with a bay window, a kitchen, two principal bedrooms, a servants' chamber and several smaller sitting rooms. At the back of the house there was a spacious garden and sun terrace, annexed by a stable for several horses.

As Caxton entered his workshop he glanced around with satisfaction. The bright whitewashed walls led up to a carved oaken roof, with the morning sun shining brightly through a narrow window, illuminating two ponderous looking machines. Caxton ran his hands over the smooth edges of the machinery, before thoughtfully picking up some individual lettering types and an ink ball. He had worked and planned meticulously for this moment; for this was his printing press. The first to be assembled in England – and would surely not be the last. Now in his early 50s, he had already led a successful life. Being the child of a wealthy merchant family who had been active members of the London Mercers Company, he had started life with obvious advantages. At the age of fifteen it had been arranged that he would become an apprentice to Robert Large, a Master of the Mercers Company and a future Mayor of London. From that point, his future career path had been assured.

Highly intelligent and shrewd, Caxton was clever enough to use this relative security as a solid base to seize opportunities when they arose, even when they had an element of risk. While still an apprentice at the age of 22, his master Robert Large had passed away, and Caxton was left to ponder his next move. He had known that in the seven years of his apprenticeship he had gained valuable business experience, and cultivated useful personal contacts. Realising that cloth had overtaken wool in export value, the young Caxton had looked towards the Low Countries in Northern Europe and particularly Bruges. Feeling sufficiently confident, he made the bold decision to depart from London to start in business by himself. The move to Bruges had proved to be immensely successful, and after completing his apprenticeship, he became a highly respected representative of the resident English business community.

By the age of 41 Caxton had been appointed Governor of the English Nation of Merchant Adventurers in the Lowlands. This was a highly paid influential position, holding real authority over his fellow merchants. This esteemed position had brought him increasingly into contact with the flamboyant court culture of the Duke and Duchess of Bergundy. Caxton's wealth of contacts had enabled him to provide the court with luxury items such as crockery, furs, silk, ermine, saffron and jewellery. At the same time he found himself being increasingly used as a representative of the Palace of Westminster, and in this capacity he became skilled in the art of diplomacy. It was while he had been residing in the leisured corridors of the court, that he cultivated a close friendship with the Duchess of Bergundy, Margaret, the sister of Edward IV. Their joint passion for literature had forged a bond that had sown the seed in Caxton's mind, and that ultimately set him on a new career path. It was when they were discussing a book written by a chaplain at the Bergundian Court, that a suggestion was made to translate it into English. William Caxton agreed to take on the task, and it was while he laboured on this project that the new technological breakthrough of printing began to concentrate his mind.

One of the men at the forefront of this revolutionary method of reproducing script was Johann Veldener in the Rhineland city of Cologne. After careful consideration, Caxton made the momentous decision to spend a year with him to learn the new craft. Veldener had proved to be a good and helpful tutor. For after Caxton had painstakingly learnt the new process, Veldener had offered practical help in establishing Caxton's press in Bruges. Now as he stood in his workshop surrounded by his machinery, Caxton recalled with deep satisfaction the day he presented the Duchess of Bergundy with a printed copy of the chaplain's book. Bound in blue velvet, he had personally dedicated it to the Duchess for her patronage and support. The manuscript had been titled *The Recuyell of the Histories of Troy* and it was his first printed book.

Caxton was suddenly brought out of this pleasant recollection by the sound of his wife's voice. Maude was informing him from the upper floor that his cousin Richard had arrived for a lunchtime appointment.

Wynkin De Worde and Richard Pynson chomped hungrily on their hot meat pies – their frenzied activity in the shop had given a keen edge to their appetites. Seated in the shop, they watched the carpenters put the finishing touches to the brackets and shelving, before they packed up their tools and left for lunch. The locality of the shop was well chosen being situated on the path leading from the King's Palace to the Abbey Church. This gave them a captive potential custom of royalty, nobility, merchants, law and churchmen. Even more importantly for two aliens working in a foreign land, Westminster was considerably less hostile than unruly London to the idea of foreign workers sharing the economy. Only the previous day, Pynson had been attacked by some London apprentices in Cornhill, his accent having fuelled their inbuilt hostility to strangers.

As they finished their pies they were confronted by a young Englishman dressed fashionably in tights and a short scarlet jacket, standing in the doorway. He introduced himself as Robert Copland, calling in relation to an advertisement circulated by Caxton the previous week. The advertisement had been circulated in both Westminster and London, requesting the need for an apprentice with literary knowledge. With two shops and a workshop, their need for more manpower if they were going to meet demand was of some urgency. Over the next 30 minutes, Copland convinced them of both his literary qualifications and his enthusiasm to learn the new technology of printing. They in turn informed Copland of how they had acquired the techniques of printing in Bruges, while working alongside their master William Caxton, and his partner Colard Mansion. Convinced of Copland's suitability, De Worde suggested he met their master, and the two men left for the short walk to the Almonry, leaving Pynson alone in the shop.

William Caxton reclined in the soft backed satin chair in his parlour, as his cousin Richard forcefully opinioned on the politics of the day. Loud and strident, Richard was never short of an opinion nor backward in expressing it. Big hearted and eager to please, he had typically arrived for lunch carrying a basket filled with asparagus and figs, that he had personally handpicked from the Abbey's gardens in Tothill Fields. William was always glad to see him, for he invariably appreciated his stimulating company and invaluable assistance. In addition to his duties as a monk in the Abbey, Richard was also a valued administrator for the Royal Palace. It had been Richard who had arranged the renting of properties in Westminster, when it had become known that William was returning to set up his printing press in the district. It had always been William's intention to return to London with his printing press at some stage, but the shifting political sands in France, and some subtle pressure from the Palace had speeded the process. Caxton had good relations with the present Yorkist King Edward IV. In addition, he was a good friend of not only the King's sister in Bergundy, but also Edward's younger brother George – the Duke of Clarence – and his present wife Queen Elizabeth Woodville and her brother Earl Rivers. Indeed, Caxton had dedicated his second printed book to the chess loving Duke of Clarence *The Game and Playe of the Chesse* while living in Bruges.

Both the Queen and her brother Earl Rivers shared a love of literature, and they had already offered patronage to Caxton. King Edward was an enthusiastic patron of the arts with a fine collection of illuminated manuscripts. Looking to add to his large library, Edward IV had followed Caxton's progress in Bruges with some interest. Caxton had in turn been much encouraged by the successful printing press he had established with his partner Colard Mansion in Bruges. It had proved to be a rewarding vocation both financially and culturally, and reports of it's success had soon reached the ears of the Palace and the

Abbey in Westminster. The popularity of reading and literature in court circles had always been a much valued pastime, but now with news of the new printing technology, interest had been further heightened. Edward soon made it known to his courtiers that he would prefer this groundbreaking facility to be closer to home. This information was promptly communicated to Caxton, with the assurance that the court would smooth his passage in the event of him returning across the channel to Westminster. Being a cousin of William, Richard had been approached in this process, and had been given assistance by the Abbot John Eastney, in finding the suitable properties for William's business.

Now the two cousins were sat enjoying their conversation, sipping the best Gascon wine out of silver cups, having sated themselves on a meal of pickled sturgeon. Their conversation turned to business when Richard mentioned that the Abbey would be prepared to pay for preprinted service sheets and Indulgencies. The fear of death and the afterlife sat permanently on the shoulders of citizens, and this anxiety provided a lucrative income for the religious order. Fuelled by the intermittent outbreaks of the plague and other diseases, people saw death as a constant companion. As was the custom with most people, the two cousins were wearing their plague pendants around their necks in order to ward of the evil scourge. Indulgencies depended on this fear of an afterlife, sold to thousands of fearful sinners by the church, they were believed to make the period of punishment in purgatory briefer. For the church, having Indulgencies printed with a blank space left for the name instead of writing them out by hand, meant that many more could be produced faster with much reduced manual toil. William Caxton estimated to Richard that he could produce nearly a thousand a day from a single press, and told him that this would be a welcome early income as he established his business. William informed his cousin that he would be visiting the Royal Court that afternoon, as he had an audience with Earl Rivers about a new business proposition. Richard expressed curiosity and good wishes before rising to his feet and embracing his cousin, his mind already turning to his busy afternoon schedule. As Caxton's wife Maude was seeing Richard off the premises, Wynkin De Worde and the young job applicant Robert Copland were approaching the house.

De Worde introduced Copland, before Maude showed them upstairs to the parlour where Caxton still sat sipping his wine. After quickly scanning the features of the young man before him, Caxton proceeded to ask questions about his background, literary knowledge, and business acumen. Copland was obviously bright, knowledgeable and energetic, and it was not long before Caxton made up his mind to employ him.

After Caxton had made it known to Copland that he was acceptable, the three men left the parlour to view the workshop. Copland was transfixed in fascination as he viewed the equipment, while Caxton and De Worde jointly explained the printing process to him. The previous day Otuel Fuller – who was a bookselling tutor from the school in the Almonry – had commissioned Caxton to print 100 copies of two popular early English childrens' books. Caxton was well familiar with the stories, as they had been the favourite childhood reading of his daughter Elizabeth. The manuscripts for these stories were piled neatly ready for printing, and as a short demonstration, De Worde operated the press as Caxton arranged some text and inked the type with an inkball. At the end of the process De Worde passed the neatly printed sheets to Copland for inspection. Copland could hardly contain his enthusiasm, as he read aloud the stylish vivid text in his hands. Caxton then went on to explain his requirements and business strategy. Richard Pynson would be stationed at the small shop in the Abbey precinct by day, and then be required to put in a shift in the workshop in the evenings. The small shop would be used only as a branch for book sales to church, nobility and law. The main bookshop at the sign of the Red Pale would house the more luxurious classical volumes, and would be mainly occupied by Caxton himself. Wynkin De Worde would be the foreman in the workshop, assisted by Copland and a Flemish compositor from Bruges who had previously been in the employ of Colard Mansion. Caxton declared that he would be the main translator of French and Bergundian texts, as it was his heartfelt aspiration to standardise the English language across the country.

Leading Copland over to the type, Caxton showed him that it was in the style of Bergundian luxury scripts, and it was in this format that he intended to print the poems of Lydgate, Gower, and that worshipful man Geoffrey Chaucer. At that precise moment Robert Copland could see that though Caxton was a shrewd buisnessman with a keen eye for profit, he could also feel his passion for literature and his intense desire for it to be shared as widely as possible. They shook hands warmly, both of them instinctively sensing a kindred spirit, before Caxton informed him that there was room for him to reside in the house as was the custom with apprentices. Copland told him that he would find that arrangement acceptable, and that he would return the next day after putting his affairs in order. After bidding Copland farewell at the door, Caxton quickly returned upstairs to ready himself for his Court visit.

Meanwhile two miles to the east, in the walled and gated City of London, the commercial life of the nation buzzed relentlessly. The population in London had slowly begun to grow again after the ravages of the Black Death and had now reached a rough approximate of 50,000. Inside the walls the overall impression was one of a busy medium sized market town, with hundreds of stalls selling fish, meat, bread, milk, honey and fruit. Among these stalls the pigs roamed freely with the cats and dogs, feeding on the offal and fruit that dropped regularly off the carts and barrows. But despite these signs of a street market economy, London had by this time become a great commercial centre and the wealthiest town in England. Already a major exporter of wool and cloth to the lowlands, London's wealth flourished further as nobles, leading churchmen, and the royal household turned to the City of London for it's luxuries. This internal demand for goods had led swiftly to London becoming a major marketplace for imported goods from Europe like fine textiles, spices, wine and furs. The wharves on the River Thames built to handle this trade, stretched from the Tower of London down to the Fleet River entrance at Blackfriars.

This thriving economic activity had proved a lucrative source of income for the London merchants and craftsmen who profited from supplying these needs. One such beneficiary of this fortunate circumstance was leading London Mercer William Pratt. It was he who now sat in a small horse driven carriage outside the Mercer's Hall and Chapel in Cheapside. It had long been the practice for men in a particular trade to band together in guilds to promote their interests, and in the case of the London Mercers had existed from the 12th century. It had grown to be one of the most powerful guilds in London, benefiting hugely from the overseas trade in wool and cloth. Along with the Merchant Taylors, the Mercers supplied nearly half of London's alderman, and had over the years provided a good share of the elected Mayors. In a state of pleasant anticipation, William Pratt instructed his coachman to proceed to Westminster; for he was going to pay a visit to his fellow Mercer and special friend William Caxton. He had known Caxton for 30 years, and had traveled to Bruges to see him for business and pleasure on numerous occasions. Likewise Caxton had visited him when in London, often enjoying lavish hospitality, and convivial evenings at his large house in Thames Street. Back in 1452 as young men, they had both ended their apprenticeships and taken the Livery of the Mercers in the same year, both simultaneously becoming Freemen of London. Pratt was well aware of the circumstances of Caxton's return to England, and being himself an enthusiastic reader of Chaucer, was now full of curiosity as to his progress. As the carriage stuttered it's way through the cluttered congestion of Cheapside, he gazed out of the window at the warehouses and shops, selling the cloth and linen he had come to know so well.

Everywhere he looked there was buying and selling, as animated faces and gestures concluded the transactions for bread, fish, poultry, silverware, saddles and shoes. Suddenly the carriage came to a halt, as up ahead a brawl had erupted between the saddler's apprentices and the poulterers. These violent outbursts were a regular occurrence in London life and could often end in bloody fatalities; but this fracas though vicious and brutal, ended swiftly with no loss of life. Eventually the carriage left the vivid colours, smells and noise of London's chief marketplace behind, and began to bear left around the magnificent Norman church of St Paul's, with it's towering spire rising 450ft above the city.

There were two main thoroughfares to Westminster; the River Thames or the fashionable highway of the Strand. William Pratt always preferred the land route, as the undulations of the river played havoc with his digestion. Approaching the outer wall of Ludgate, William Pratt reached for a silk handkerchief and put it to his nose. For they were in the vicinity of the open sewer that was officially known as the River Fleet, and that was now emitting it's usual obnoxious stink. Passing through the gate they entered the newly created ward of Farringdon Without – further evidence of London's increasing expansion to the west. As the carriage picked up apace along Fleet Street, William examined the contents of a large white cloth bag that he had brought with him on his journey. As a wealthy merchantman, it was never difficult for him to obtain the more original luxury items that traded across the channel. He felt the selection of items in his bag would provide good presents for the Caxton family, as well as amusement and curiosity.

Passing through Temple Bar, they were now out of the City of London's jurisdiction. Entering the Strand, he never failed to be fascinated by the continuous ribbon of Bishop's Inns that stretched along the entire south side. The abundant wealth of the church was well reflected in these grand structures, and William Pratt was duly impressed. The notable exception to all this opulence was the once magnificent Savoy Palace, now standing desolate, damaged and empty.

It had been attacked and badly damaged by Wat Tyler's followers in the Peasants Revolt 100 years earlier, and up to now had languished in pathetic disrepair. To his right was a vast expanse of pasture, occasionally interrupted by a small cluster of dwellings. The autumn afternoon was cool and clear, causing him to draw his fur coat tightly around him. Entering the small village of Charing, William recognised the houses belonging to some of his rich merchant friends, for it was a popular area for the rich and successful. The carriage passed the Royal Mews, where some of the finest horses in the land were fed and watered, and were chiefly used by Edward IV for Royal Pageants and hunting activities. They then passed the last of the Queen Eleanor memorial crosses, erected by Edward I some 200 years previous in memory of his beloved wife.

At this point the main road swung to the right, leading through the fields to Knightsbridge; but instead of following this route the carriage veered left to take the muddy track that led to Westminster. It had been six months since William Pratt had last seen Caxton in his print shop in Bruges, and at that time there had been no clue that Caxton would soon be returning to England. On his visit to Caxton's shop he had been both fascinated and impressed by the new printing process, but also surprised that Caxton had taken up such a challenging vocation at this stage in his life. He had rarely seen his friend so enthused, but after meeting his printing partner Colard Mansion, he saw the same fervent glint in the eyes and began to understand. After Pratt returned to London, he began to hear conversations in the Mercers Hall that Caxton would soon be returning to Westminster with his printing press, and much to his delight it had come to pass. His contacts in the Hall had given him the information regarding Caxton's residence at the Almonry, so he had taken it upon himself to pay a visit to his old friend as soon as possible. Looking out of the window to his right, he could now see the fields and gardens belonging to the Abbott of Westminster, before passing through the barren stretch of land called 'Scotland' named after Adam Scot, who once owned the district some 200 years before. Just as the road narrowed and became King Street, they passed the impressive residence of the Archbishop of York. With it's immaculate gardens leading down to the River Thames; York Place was one of the most desirable properties owned by the church. As the carriage entered the Westminster village William Pratt never failed to be stirred by the feeling of power and industry, as the governing classes rushed about their business involving important matters of state. As they approached the Almonry Gate, the small congregated groups of the shiftless and the deserving poor gazed on curiously. The carriage finally came to a halt under the sign of the Red Pale, and William Pratt glanced up at the familiar Heraldic shield, before alighting from the carriage holding his large white bag tightly to his chest.

On his way to the Royal Palace, Willliam Caxton had looked in on his small shop near the Chapter House. Richard Pynson and Wynkin De Worde were still making themselves busy, as they stacked the shelves and categorised the stock. Caxton was pleased at their progress, and expressed his satisfaction with the overall advancement of the project. Caxton then informed them of his appointment with Earl Rivers, before bidding his farewell and proceeding across the Palace Yard. Threading his way through the crowds, he crossed a small yard before turning into a narrow alley leading to a solid medium sized building. Entering an arched entrance, he was confronted by an armoured guard who demanded his name and the nature of his business. After informing the guard of both his name and the planned meeting with Earl Rivers, Caxton was led through a series of small passages into a spacious gallery. It was a routine in that William Caxton had become very familiar, and he was soon seating himself in one of the chairs that were randomly arranged around the room. As he waited for his audience with Earl Rivers, Caxton studied the small groups of gathered courtiers as they murmured to each other in low voices. Some of them were huddled together in pairs playing chess or draughts, while the more solitary among them immersed themselves in books and paperwork. It was said that Edward IV had reduced his Court population from the extravagant excesses of the previous King Henry VI. Nevertheless it was still estimated to hold approximately 600 staff in total, including kitchen staff, clerks, grooms, musicians, and pages, in addition to the knights and esquires who attended the King. After the trials and tribulations of the Wars of the Roses, the Royal Palace was enjoying a period of calm and stability. Edward IV had fought long and hard for the Yorkist cause, showing great courage and determination against the Lancastrian Henry. At last he was now in a position to make good his promises, fulfilling the pledges that had gained him his subjects' support, and the London merchants in particular. Henry's policy of preferential export licences to Italians, and his repeated desertions of London in times of danger, turned the London business community against him. Edward's promise to reverse these measures, and restore London's rightful place as the centre of government, had ensured that London and it's merchants had backed the House of York. The merchants knew all too well that the power of the Royal Court to attract men of wealth and ambition from across the land, would ensure that Westminster would become an enormous driving force in London's prosperity. As a result, men like Caxton and his fellow London merchants had already made a rich living by providing the Court with the assorted luxuries that they demanded. As Caxton sat waiting in the gallery, his relaxed and serene demeanour occasionally attracted curious glances from the huddled courtiers. For in the Courtiers constant search for advancement and Royal favour above their rivals, they were vulnerable to feelings of insecurity and suspicion of strangers. William Caxton's thoughts turned to his appointment with Earl Rivers, as he contemplated the possible nature of his business proposition. He had already been assured of Earl Rivers patronage, so he assumed it must be connected to some literary venture. Minutes later Caxton was summoned by a page and shown into a spacious room just off the gallery, it's walls richly decorated in elaborate tapestries.

Walking towards the seated Earl Rivers, Caxton gently bowed before accepting the Earl's invitation to take a seat opposite.

The Earl was in many ways an arrogant, vain and conceited man, but Caxton also knew that there was a more sensitive side to his nature, with an almost childlike eagerness to please, and a desperation to be liked. The Earl briefly enquired of Caxton's progress in the setting up of his press, before immediately setting out the nature of his proposal. Having been appointed by Edward IV to be Governor to his six-year-old son Edward, the Prince of Wales, it was the duty of Earl Rivers to educate the young future King in the arts and the English language. Earl Rivers went on to explain that with this responsibility in mind, he had identified two

Bergundian Classic stories that had been personal favourites of his, and of that Caxton was well familiar. The first story was *History of Jason* a tale that dealt in chivalric romance and heroic deeds, and was sure to please the King. Earl Rivers was prepared to advance a considerable sum of money to Caxton, not only for it's translation into English, but also for a significant bulk order once the book was printed. The second story was *Dicts of the Philosophers* a collection of sayings passed down through the ages professing wisdom, understanding and virtue. Earl Rivers then surprised Caxton by expressing a desire to attempt to translate the story into English himself, with a view to Caxton overseeing his work for amendments before printing. Earl Rivers had obviously calculated that to attempt and fulfill such a project, would give him much esteem in the Court, and be much appreciated by the King. William Caxton was more than happy to collaborate on this joint venture, and he quickly worked out the details in terms of timing and finance. Their business concluded satisfactorily, Earl Rivers escorted Caxton back out to the gallery, before bidding his farewell and returning whence he had come. As William Caxton prepared to leave the gallery, there was a slight commotion among the courtiers, as the tall figure of the King followed by his entourage entered the passage. After all the battles and tribulations the King was now enjoying the trappings of royalty, and as he passed by the fawning courtiers, he exuded a relaxed and easy charm. Upon seeing Caxton bow, he smiled and nodded recognition, before passing on through the hallway and into the chapel. William Caxton admired and liked the King for his commendable qualities of bravery, intelligence and graciousness, but above all for his commitment to the arts and his personal interest in his project. Pleased and satisfied with the day's events, Caxton turned towards the narrow staircase that led to the exit gate.

William Pratt had been given a warm welcome by Maude Caxton and her daughter Elizabeth, when he had arrived unexpectedly at the Almonry residence earlier. He was now reclining in the parlour, contentedly supping ale from a pewter mug, and engaged in convivial conversation with Maude and her daughter. He had been informed of William Caxton's appointment at the Court, with the welcome news that his friend was not expected to be too long in returning. Maude had been most insistent that he should stay for supper, and that he should defer till the morning his return to his Thames Street house.

When William Caxton eventually returned, there was much backslapping and gentle teasing between the two men. Their friendship through the years, and the pleasant recollections of common experience that that attachment had forged, had bonded the two Mercers in comfortable familiarity. After Caxton had wasted no time in exhibiting to his friend the printing press and the workshop, he then escorted William Pratt to the small shop at the Chapter House in the Abbey Precinct. De Worde and Pynson had both met Caxton's friend on the previous occasion in Bruges, and they stood aside with some satisfaction as Pratt admired the shelves stacked with ordered books. On his way back from the Palace earlier, Caxton had informed the two men of the business arrangement with Earl Rivers. Wynkin De Worde had in turn relayed to Caxton the welcome news that the small shop would be open and ready for business come the morrow.

After returning to the Almonry house, William Pratt and the Caxton family had congregated in the parlour before dinner. Suddenly in the middle of the general conversation, William Pratt produced his white cloth bag with a dramatic flourish, and announced it was time for some interesting gifts. Immediately intrigued, William, Maude and Elizabeth gathered round as Pratt rummaged through the bag and carefully laid out the contents. On the table before them were two wooden cups bound with silver gilt, two gold necklaces, two silk purses, six silver spoons and a luxury pack of hand painted playing cards. Both Maude and Elizabeth could hardly conceal their delight, as they enthusiastically scrutinized the items and passed them between themselves. William Pratt had deliberately held back one last article, which he now carefully withdrew from the bag. Placing a high quality wooden chessboard on the table, he then proceeded to place the pieces in their appropriate positions in deliberate fashion.

With a delighted shout, William Caxton immediately moved forward and studied the pieces. Caxton could see that they had been hand carved from walrus ivory, with the seated figures intricately carved with floral and animal designs. Through the years Caxton had seen many fine chess sets, but the one laid out before him easily surpassed all others. The game of chess had been an enduring interest of Caxton's for as long as he could remember, and as in most things he indulged, he had become quite an accomplished player. William Pratt had been on the receiving end of this expertise on more than one occasion, and had obviously seen the set as a suitable gift. William Caxton could not begin to imagine how his friend had come by such a handsome example of the genre, but knowing that information for such an original item had to be volunteered, he advanced towards Pratt and settled for a grateful embrace. Pleased with the response to his gifts, William Pratt noted

Caxton's quizzical expression and decided to satisfy his friends curiosity. He enlightened Caxton by telling him that the chess set had been made by an English craftsman skilled in the style of Viking art, and it had ended up in the hands of a rich Goldsmith in Cheapside. The Goldsmith had given him the Chess Set as part of a deal for some gold chains and other jewellery.

Later on in the candlelit dining room, they all hungrily feasted on a supper of pheasant and asparagus. The subject of the coming Mayoral elections came up for discussion, with the two Mercers evaluating the prospects for their guild's candidate. Always held at the end of October on the feast of St Simon and St Jude, it was the most important civic event of the year, and both of them would be expected to attend. On the special day, the newly elected Mayor would be transported from the city along the River Thames to Westminster in a splendid state barge. Following on behind would be the river craft in the full livery of the various guilds, arranged in order of importance. It was a matter of special consequence to the guilds to have their due appropriate place in the procession, and it caused just as much rivalry among the Mercers, Goldsmiths, Merchant Taylors and Skinners, as the election of the Mayor itself. At the table, Maude voiced her anxiety that she hoped the occasion would not be marred as it was the year before, by rival apprentices brawling in the streets. After sharing her concerns, the two Mercers rose from the table holding their goblets of Gascony Claret, and retreated to the parlour.

Some time later all was peaceful, as an air of tranquility settled on the Westminster Village. The two friends sat crouched over the chess board in the flickering candlelight, both men totally absorbed as they wrestled with the options presented by the 64 squares. The only sounds that could be heard were the occasional spitting emissions of the wood burning in the fire, and the soft spiritual voices of the choir in the Abbey. After a careful and guarded opening, the contest had proceeded to the middle game with good tempo and development, leaving both players with fully equal prospects. At one stage traveling on the evening air, they heard the muted distant bells from inside the walls at Ludgate, signaling the 9 o'clock curfew and the closing of the gates. The serenity was suddenly broken by a gasp of resignation from a rueful William Pratt, as he rose from the table and offered his hand to Caxton. He had launched what he had hoped to be an overwhelming assault, but Caxton had defended it well, and saw the chance to counter with a sustained attack that had proved to be decisive and winning. The two men chuckled genially as they moved their chairs nearer to the fire, taking the opportunity to refill their goblets with claret. Caxton again thanked his friend for his generous gifts, before promising to give him his first printed copy of Chaucer's *Canterbury Tales*. William Pratt was overjoyed with this offering, as the story had long been his favourite reading matter.

Suddenly looking pensive, William Pratt thought it best to inform Caxton that his printing press was not without it's detractors at the Mercers Hall. Caxton looked questioningly at his friend, before encouraging him to continue. His manner slightly hesitant, Pratt expanded the theory that some merchants thought that too much widespread knowledge among the poor, could lead to dissatisfaction and civil unrest. William Caxton pondered this possibility, before answering that he really had no time for such narrow minded prejudice, for he saw it as his duty that the work of men like Chaucer should be available to everyone, and passed down for posterity. With his expression hardening in the flickering firelight, he went on to say that if his printing was wrong, then it was a fine and noble wrong. After being informed by Caxton that it was his intention to put in print all of Chaucer's works, William Pratt offered the business proposition that it be a joint venture with himself. His offer was that by paying a competitive rate for a sizable number of copies in advance, Caxton could do a larger print run and he could sell them privately to interested customers. William Caxton did not deliberate long before accepting his friend's offer, signaling his acceptance by refilling their drinking vessels and hailing the King. It was close to midnight as the two friends rose unsteadily from their chairs. They had talked long into the night and they were now ready for slumber. It was just after they had embraced and moved towards their sleeping quarters in the dimly lit narrow corridor, that a sudden thought occurred to William Pratt. Turning round to Caxton, he sounded anxious as he asked 'What if there are two many books printed for too few readers?' William Caxton thought for a moment before smiling and answering, 'There is no cause for concern my friend, for it is books that make readers'.

2

LONDON
JUNE 1599

The River Thames is running at high tide, gently lapping the shores and rocking the ships, making their timbers creak. The swans upon the river glide in rhythm with the undulating surface. What remains of the moonlight casts a silvery luminous glow over the Tower of London, as the first signs of an early morning mist begin to emerge, revealing the promise of a hot summers day. Rural sounds come from the sheep already queuing at the London Bridge gate on the Southwark side. Having been herded through the night from the Kent pastures, only to be confronted with their meat market destiny.

There is the faint melodious sound of a Lute, being played in an open window in one of the houses on the Bridge. On the city side a few lights were beginning to show in the windows, gradually the sky begins to turn blue and the stars gently fade. London was awakening.

On a balcony overlooking the Thames on Bankside, Southwark – witnessing this scene – stood a thoughtful balding man in his late thirties. His name was William Shakespeare. Throughout the night he had been both restless and excited, his brain running through the lines of his latest play *Julius Caesar*. The play was to be performed that coming day in the official opening of his newly built theatre The Globe. That morning as he gazed across the Thames he had plenty to reflect on. The gamble of leaving his wife and children back in his home town of Stratford-Upon-Avon 13 years earlier, had paid off on a massive scale. The irresistible compulsion that had driven him to join an acting troop and come to London, was something that in retrospect as an otherwise practical man, he could not rationalise.

But there was no denying that his actions had brought him and his family great wealth and renown, giving him the opportunity to fully realise his genius as a playwright. As he gazed across the river towards the city, he knew with every fibre of his being that it could not have been possible without London. In the course of those 13 years he had come to know London very well, and likewise London had come to know him. Widely recognised by his neighbours and the citizens who crowded the public theatres, he was continually hailed and greeted in the streets and taverns. He in turn knew the bookshops of St Paul's Churchyard and Paternoster Row, where he would spend hours fueling his imagination with the printed word. He knew the taverns where the finest wines were sold, and the inns where the best beers and ales were provided. He had a connoisseur's knowledge of the best eating houses on both sides of the river. In the summer he was a frequent visitor to the Royal Exchange on Sunday afternoons, taking the opportunity to enjoy the free concerts that were regularly staged. He crossed the Thames continually by ferry and was familiar with all the moods of the river, and perhaps imperative to his drama, he knew the dark side of London and all that entailed. As the daybreak finally arrived, he turned away from the river and returned to his rooms. For there was much work to be done – and time was at a premium.

Richard Quiney had also risen early that morning after a restless night. He had been kept awake by some pressing financial concerns that needed to be resolved. Leaving his London lodgings at the Bell Inn in Carter Lane, he stepped out into the rapidly warming daylight. He proceeded to walk through St Paul's Churchyard on his way to his regular barber in Cheapside. As he reclined in the barbers chair enjoying a shave, the subject of the Globe Theatre seemed to be the topical event of the day among the clientele, and was causing some excitement. The conversation was of some interest to him, for it was his intention to attend the official opening of the newly built playhouse that afternoon. The reason for this was twofold; he was a lifelong friend of William Shakespeare, and more importantly their home town of Stratford-Upon-Avon was in financial difficulties. The two of them had grown up together forming a bond that was deep and lasting. As boys, they had both hunted hares and foxes in the vast expanse of fields surrounding their home town, and shared days angling together on the River Avon. They both shared the experience of having father's who were respected businessmen who knew each other well, and who both rose to become the Mayor of Stratford-Upon-Avon. William Shakespeare was godfather to Richard's son William, whom Richard had named in honour to his highly acclaimed friend. Like Shakespeare, Richard had also found London to his liking, establishing a successful career as a London based merchant, eventually serving the interests of his Avon home town by ensuring that export/import trade flowed between the two towns on a regular basis. Attaining the status of Alderman of Stratford-Upon-Avon, the funds needed to sustain his advocacy of Stratford's business in the capital were beginning to dry up, as a succession of bad harvests had weakened the financial strength of the town. It was his intention that day to approach his old friend after the performance, in order to gain some financial assistance and make him fully aware of their home town's plight.

William Shakespeare dressed himself methodically and neatly, as he always did, showing great attention to detail. His clothes were regularly cleaned and dried at the Moor Fields laundries by the acting companies laundresses, and then delivered back to him stacked in orderly fashion. Because it was hot he wore an open neck shirt with a big collar, breeches down to the knees, silk stockings, with highly coloured leather shoes completing the apparel. He studied himself in a mirror made of polished steel. His chiseled features were still in evidence, though middle-age was approaching fast. A small earring and a neatly trimmed moustache were his only facial adornments.

His lodgings on Bankside, Southwark, near the Clink prison, suited him perfectly. Being one of the larger houses in that area overlooking the River Thames, he had the facility of two rooms and a riverside balcony, plus the added advantage of being close to the centre of all his activities. Though not the most salubrious of areas, Southwark had for many years been associated with public entertainment; chiefly because of the city authorities insistence that lewd, cruel, and violent activities should be played out well away from the city centre. The area had become well known for bull-fighting and bear-baiting. This blood thirsty recreation was a peculiar love of the English, and conducted with a ferocity that horrified continental visitors. The Bear Garden was close by, and Shakespeare would often hear the screeching death throes, and smell the reek of the animals on a daily basis. Shakespeare was well aware that he lived in an area that was characterized by violence and casual cruelty, but he was also inspired by its colourful liveliness and youthful energy. Because of this, Southwark was something of an actors' district; indeed two of his acting colleagues from his theatrical company – The Lord Chamberlains Men – lived alongside him on the river. Their names were Thomas Pope and Augustine Philipps, and along with Shakespeare, were part of the five man consortium helping to fund the Globe project. The project had materialised after the Company had lost its theatre in Shoreditch north of the river. After consulting with the Burbage brother's Richard and Cuthbert, who were the theatrical company owners, Shakespeare had discussed a proposition with four other members of the acting troop. They agreed to help finance the building of the new theatre in Southwark, and to split any profits that ensued. Shakespeare stepped out into the bright warm sunlight, and walked towards the Globe theatre a few hundred yards away.

Richard Quiney handed over two pennies for his haircut and shave, before stepping out into Cheapside, where the bright sunshine seemed to have awakened the city earlier than was usual. Cheapside was already swamped with street-traders hustling and jostling, creating a sea of continuous noise as arguments and street-selling dominated the senses. Quiney dodged his way through the melee, passing the tall Cheapside houses with ornately decorated exteriors owned by the Goldsmiths. These fine buildings existed alongside the variety of merchant premises where the owners stood in their doorways, eager to bargain with potential customers. There were rows of shops with metal signs that creaked and swung, selling cheeses, pickles, gloves, herbs, spices, and sacks of corn. Avoiding the old women crouched upon the ground with parcels of nuts, or withered vegetables, were the endless numbers of men carrying sacks on their backs, and the children wheeling barrows calling out for trade. Quiney eventually got back to his lodgings in Carter Lane. Once inside his first floor room, the contrast with the outside hubbub was stark and welcome. He sat at a desk and opened a heavy leather bound journal, calculating that he had an hour or so before lunch to complete some of his formidable accounting work. He reached for his quill pen and set to his business.

William Shakespeare swelled with both pride and excitement as the Globe came into his view. It was already considered to be the most splendid of all the London theatres in terms of its design and appearance. It had not been an easy construction; strong foundations had to be laid, since it was erected on marshy grasslands, with wooden piles being driven deep into the soggy Southwark soil. The Globe's structure was of oak timber, polygonal in shape, accommodating some fourteen sides, with three galleries surrounding the stage and the open pit. The playhouse was 100 feet in diameter, with a capacity to hold

3,300 tightly packed Elizabethan bodies. It's exterior was daubed in white plaster with an open thatched roof. Shakespeare crossed the man made bridge over the surrounding ditch to gain access.

Once inside he immediately noticed his actor friends, Pope and Philipps, along with the two other actors who had made up the consortium – Will Kempe and John Heminges. They welcomed him warmly, as he joined in with their efforts to erect a canopy on two wooden pillars above the stage. This apparatus was decorated with stars and planets on a celestial blue background, and was known as the 'Heavens'. The stage itself was just under 50ft in width, surrounded by vividly coloured paintings and intricate carvings with much gilt and gold, the overall result being one of ornate grandeur.

There was much frenzied activity and noise as the preparations began to dominate proceedings, and on the balcony above the stage there were already a group of musicians practicing on trumpets, drums, horns and lutes. Various checks and preparations were being enacted, the trapdoor on the stage that enabled the actors to ascend and descend as if by magic, was being oiled and checked. Bladders of sheep's blood were being stacked for the murder and battle scenes. Fireworks, squibs and smoke bombs, were being prepared to simulate both cannon fire and thunderstorms. All around the stage lighted candles were being placed behind bottles of coloured water, in order to provide malevolent ambience. The actors knew that the Elizabethan audiences insisted on colour and exhibition, so the stage had to be the focus of communal allurement. The play was due to begin at 3 o'clock that afternoon with a capacity crowd expected. Playbills advertising the forthcoming entertainment had been pasted on walls and posts all around London.

The Lord Chamberlains Men theatrical company had been together in it's present form for five years. The five man consortium, plus company manager Richard Burbage, and his brother Cuthbert, were a close knit group of actors who were also intimate friends, so there was much cheerful wit and banter as they set about their tasks. Being the author of the play, Shakespeare produced the official play-book, and began to run through various set plays and rehearsals with the players. Augustine Pope, who was also an accomplished musician, was organising the arrangements with the players assembled on the balcony. There was much noise and laughter coming from William Kempe. He was the most famous and versatile comic actor in the country; small and stout, quick and nimble, he was also known for his variety of dance. Amidst much merriment, he was structuring the choreography for the numerous dance routines that complimented the narrative. At 12 o'clock Shakespeare hoisted a flag to be flown from the roof. This announced that the playhouse was now officially open, and a trumpet was blown to alert those in the vicinity.

Richard Quiney laid down his quill, closed his journal and rubbed his eyes. Rising from the desk he walked across to the window that overlooked the busy thoroughfare that was Carter Lane. The population of London had more than doubled to 175,000 people in the last century, most of them attracted to it's vibrant wealthy economy. The Bell Inn had been Quiney's London lodgings for as long as he could remember. It had suited his purposes, and he still preferred to reside there even though his personal wealth had grown considerably in that time. Looking out of the window at the London skyline, he mused on the fact that now he was a successful merchant, his network of contacts in the commercial world stretched all over the city. Quiney realised that he had been lucky in catching the wave of economic prosperity that had flowered in Elizabethan London at that time. For timing was indeed everything. Thinking of his friend William Shakespeare, he realised that this was the case in the Bard's fortunes too, with the boom in theatrical entertainment coming at just the right time. Was it fated to be, or was it just pure good fortune? Looking down on the busy street, he saw the numerous beggars with arms outstretched. Could that have easily been him? How indiscriminate were the arrows of life's misfortunes. Just how fragile was the line between prosperity and desolation? The present plight of his home town brought this question sharply into focus.

A sudden tapping on the door snapped him out of this revelry. Upon answering, Quiney was confronted by the bailiff of Stratford, Abraham Sturley, an acquaintance of many years. It had been Sturley who had originally written to him, laying out in some detail the economic difficulties that had befallen his hometown. Sturley explained to Quiney that he had took the opportunity to visit him, while in London on some other business. After Quiney had invited him to sit down, Sturley asked him if there had been any progress as regards extra finance for the Stratford Corporation. Quiney proceeded to tell him of his plan to approach William Shakespeare that very day, and then invited Sturley to dine with him in the downstairs eating quarters. The Proprietor of the Bell Inn was a big cheerful man who had known Richard Quiney many years. Their relationship was based on mutual interest, reinforced with a genuine affection that had grown through the years. Quiney had provided good contacts for the Inn in terms of linen, cooking equipment, and foodstuffs. The proprietor in turn had always ensured that Quiney was provided with the best that the Inn could offer, in terms of comfort, food and privacy. After a genial conversation between the two about the warmth of the day, and the opening of the Globe Theatre, the proprietor showed the two men to Quiney's favourite table in the far corner of the tavern. The Inn was busy as usual, and the two of them had trouble making themselves heard above the din, as they ordered chicken and bacon, to be washed down with a Corsican wine. For the next hour the two men were heavily engrossed in conversation, as the ambience and hospitality of the establishment lightened the seriousness of their business. Finally rising from the table, they bid their farewells in the bright hot sunshine outside the Inn. Quiney immediately headed south towards the river, for it was his intention to take a ferry from Blackfriars across to the Paris Garden Pier in Southwark.

On the Southwark side there was a steady stream of humanity heading towards the Theatre, making their way through the packed tenements, swarming streets, stable yards and alleys. Inside the Theatre, William Shakespeare watched with satisfaction as the richer Londoners and their ladies began to fill the upper galleries. As for this opening performance, the price had been doubled to four pence for those wishing to reside in the balconies. Suddenly Shakespeare's attention was drawn to the sound of raised voices coming from behind the stage. Several of the actors rushed immediately to the source of the fracas, with Shakespeare arriving just in time to see his friend and manager Richard Burbage, being held forcibly against the wall. Upon looking at the attacker. Shakespeare instantly recognised the small shabby figure of Giles Allen, their old landlord from the Shoreditch Theatre. With the aid of William Kempe, Burbage managed to disentangle himself from Allen's clutches. The cause of the hostility between the two men had a long history, and was the catalyst for the building of the Globe Theatre. With the outstanding success of the Shoreditch playhouse, Giles Allen had sought to vastly improve his profit margins by practically doubling the ground rent. He had also demanded that the theatre should be his property after a five year period. Shakespeare and Burbage were never going to agree with such an arrangement, and after scrutinizing the wording on the existing contract very carefully, they discovered what seemed like a crucial loophole.

Giles Allen had seemed to own the land where the theatre was built, but he did not have ownership rights on the theatre under the present arrangement. So the Lord Chamberlains men embarked on the radical solution of dismantling the theatre beam by beam, and then shipping the building materials across the River Thames to be stored in Southwark. Giles Allen had obviously been surprised and angered by this wanton vandalism of his cash cow, and had instantly sued Richard Burbage and his brother Cuthbert, £800 for damages. As William Kempe restrained a struggling Giles Allen that early afternoon, the reason for Allen's aggressive behaviour quickly became apparent to Shakespeare. It transpired that Allen had just left the offices of his legal representation, having been given the unwelcome news that he was due no compensation. The legal verdict was that the Lord Chamberlain's men were quite within their rights, and that they had behaved within the strict interpretation of the law. Eventually a dejected Giles Allen was escorted off the premises, as Shakespeare and the rest of the company assured themselves of Richard Burbage's well being. Within minutes they were back to the business of preparation, for there was a play to be performed, and they had lost vital time.

The interest that was generated by the opening of the Globe was building in momentum, with the hot summer weather seeming to add to the sense of excitement and occasion. Hundreds of porters, carters, and apprentices, from the numerous trades and businesses, were taking the afternoon off to see the grand opening. There were masses of people lining the north bank of the Thames, waiting to be ferried across to Southwark. Ferrymen were everywhere – the surface of the river was black with craft. There were about 3,000 watermen that plied their trade on the river, using a variety of vessels, including wherries, tide-boats, tilt-boats and hoys. The air was filled with their renowned vile and abusive language, as they competed with each other for custom. When Richard Quiney finally reached the crowds at Blackfriars, he quickly realised that his chances of getting a ferry to Paris Garden in time for the performance were extremely slim. After pausing momentarily, he turned eastwards along Thames Street in the direction of London Bridge. To his right as he walked, there was a network of narrow streets leading down to the river, at the end of these streets he could hear the shouts of the ferryman and passengers on the jetty steps. As he neared London Bridge a strong smell of fish pervaded his nostrils.

Fish Street Market was the main approach to London Bridge and the heat of the day had made the stench more formidable. Quickening his step through the thronging masses, he approached the Northern Gates of London Bridge. On reaching the crossing, Quiney was confronted with the usual intractable traffic problems, as the milling mass of humanity competed with the Kent farmers herding their cattle and flocks of sheep. London Bridge was the only way to cross the river with carts and livestock, and was a marvel of mediaeval construction, with beautiful buildings on both sides owned by rich merchants who kept their shops on the ground floors. As Quiney shuffled through the melee, he had plenty of time to admire the four story structures, the Renaissance arches, gilded columns and carved galleries, that dominated the shop fronts. There were some occasional gaps between the houses where he could glimpse a view of the Tower of London to his left, and the distant flag above the Globe Theatre to his right.

Passing under the Great Stone Gateway at the end of the Bridge on the Southwark Bank, Quiney glanced up to see the grinning decomposing skulls of traitors heads. These were displayed as a constant reminder to all good citizens that Elizabethan Britain should never be challenged. As Quiney passed through Southwark market opposite the impressive imposing structure of Southwark Cathedral, there were the constant cries of the street sellers ringing in his ears. Fish wives, selling oysters as well as fish in baskets, fruit sellers, sausage and onion sellers, all played a part in the commercial activity of London. Feeling hot and sweaty, Quiney purchased a baked apple codling for sustenance, all the while looking out for the numerous sneak thieves and pickpockets that preyed on the distracted crowds outside the playhouses.

On arriving at the Theatre entrance, Quiney threaded his way through the crowds. Paying his four pennies, he was guided towards the raised galleries, away from the rowdy atmosphere that was growing in the pit. Quiney seated himself on a wooden bench, squeezing himself in between the tightly packed nobility of London life. In the build up to the play there were many sellers among the crowd, with oranges, apples, nuts, and bottled beer being purchased, while the stench and noise of the crowd created its own overpowering ambience. There was some delay to the proceedings due to some late arrivals, this caused some nuts and fruit to be hurled at the stage from the volatile porters and apprentices that were tightly assembled in the pit. Then suddenly there were three loud bangs followed by some stirring music. Will Kempe seemed to make his entrance from outside the Theatre, vaulting onto the stage and turning a somersault, before announcing the play had begun. The actors then appeared and disappeared at regular intervals, the speech and the action being performed at great speed, creating an illusion of a flowing imaginative world. The elaborate colourful costumes of the actors dazzled vividly in the hot afternoon sunshine, as they interacted repeatedly with the crowd in between the frequent musical and dramatic episodes. In the following two hours, Quiney was to experience feelings of both excitement and apprehension, mixed in with bouts of amused laughter and morbid sadness.

At the end of the play, the noise was tumultuous as the next date of performance was announced, upon which there were appreciative cries for the author of the play. Suddenly there appeared Quiney's lifelong friend William Shakespeare, rising from the trap-door, now dressed in a crimson cape draped over one shoulder, with a tall hat and sword completing the ensemble. Bowing to the cheering crowd he was joined on stage by the complete cast of actors, as they milked the applause and bantered with the apprentices in the pit. There then followed the ritual prayers for the monarch, when all the actors knelt upon the stage. The performance finally ended with the stage jig, which was a comical musical afterpiece in which all of the actors joined in. After that there was a scrambled exodus, as many of the spectators wanted to carry on the party in the numerous inns and taverns that surrounded the Playhouse.

Quiney stayed seated on his bench, patiently waiting for the crowd to clear, all the while keeping an eye out for his friend. Finally making his way down to the stage area, he caught the attention of John Heminges, one of the actors whom he had met on several occasions in the company of Shakespeare. After warm greetings, Heminges informed Quiney that Shakespeare had already left the Theatre and was taking refreshments in The Elephant, an inn just a few yards from the Globe. Quiney uttered his gratitude and wasted no time in completing the short walk to the inn. Once inside, Quiney was confronted with a boisterous mix of noise, oppressive heat, and stale bodies.

After initially finding it difficult to spot his old friend, he was luckily seen by Shakespeare and hailed heartily. Shakespeare was in a good mood, the opening of the Globe, plus the response to his new play, could hardly have gone better. They had played to a full house and were already in profit, and now he was enjoying the euphoric afterglow among his friends and admirers. Quiney gave his friend warm praise and congratulations, before hinting that he had come to see him on some serious business regarding their home town. Shakespeare saw the earnestness in his friend's eyes and suggested they should address it later that evening, in the meantime inviting Quiney to drink copiously from a jug laden with ale.

The warm early evening and exulted atmosphere enhanced the celebrations, and it was only the church bells of London ringing in the

9 o'clock curfew that ended the revelry. After much hugging and back slapping farewells with his fellow actors, Shakespeare left the inn with Quiney for the short walk back to his lodgings. The big house was one of the properties owned by his actor friend Augustine Phillips, with Shakespeare occupying the two rooms upstairs. On entering the premises Shakespeare cheerfully requested the resident housemaid to prepare some oysters and wine, while inviting Quiney to sit down and make himself comfortable. After they had eaten their oysters and caught up on family gossip, Quiney had laid out in meticulous detail the present financial plight of their home town. In the silence that followed, the two friends sat opposite each other quietly reflective and deep in thought. Around them the candlelight danced its reflection on the rich tapestries that decorated the surrounding walls. Shakespeare had known that times had been hard in Stratford, indeed he had noticed on his last visit two months before that the prosperous buzzing town of his youth seemed strangely subdued. His wife Anne had hinted that certain families in the town were struggling with their daily existence in terms of finance. Shakespeare himself had benefitted from the property slump in Stratford, having recently purchased several houses in the high street on attractive terms. What he had not realised was the scale of the hardship. Quiney had asked for a loan of £30 on behalf of the Stratford Corporation led by the bailiff of Stratford, Abraham Sturley, a man that Shakespeare knew and respected. For Sturley to request such a loan suggested the gravity of the problems, and of course it was in Shakespeare's interest to help Stratford thrive, his family and property interests guaranteed that to be the case.

After much deliberation Shakespeare told Quiney that he would like to help, but that in matters of finance his head would always rule his heart. He told Quiney that he would arrange a money lender of his acquaintance, to loan the money at a competitive rate within a generous time frame. Quiney nodded his gratitude as they rose from the table and embraced, before moving outside to the balcony overlooking the River Thames. The water lapped gently on the riverbanks as the warm starlit night gradually darkened. A distant bark from a dog and an occasional spirited song from a late night reveler, were the only sounds that now interfered with the serenity that was descending over London. The large Gothic structure that was St Paul's Cathedral loomed large in the skyline, as the lights flickered in the thousands of windows that were facing them. They both loved this great city, it had been unusually kind to them. They proceeded to talk of this good fortune and much more long into the night. Quiney finally yawned and retired to a spare bed made up for him earlier by the housemaid, leaving Shakespeare alone on the balcony. The troubling news of his home town that Quiney had relayed, made Shakespeare realise that in future he would have to divide his time more evenly between his two favourite towns. Eventually for the sake of his family's future welfare, Stratford would demand more priority. With the sudden stark sobering realisation that there would come a time when London would no longer be pivotal to his life, he turned slowly away from the Thames with a heavy heart.

3

LONDON
SEPTEMBER 1666

The late summer sun began to appear in the eastern sky, chasing away the misty gloom of the early morning. Signs of life began to appear all along the busy highway that was the River Thames. At the same time the intricate network of narrow streets and alleys that so characterised Reformation London, began to hum with human traffic. A strong warm easterly breeze created clouds of dust in the streets, stifling the atmosphere, and causing the early morning sun to haze. Thomas Farriner stood in the doorway of his bake house in Pudding Lane wiping the sweat from his brow, he swilled deeply from a mug of beer to help quench his thirst. Being the King's baker his main duty was to provide the ship's biscuit for the fleet, but he also made a good profit selling bread to the inns and taverns from his small shop. Finishing his beer, Thomas walked up a side street before turning into the churchyard of St Margeret's. Even before she came into his view he could hear the despairing sobs of his wife Elizabeth. Walking around the side of the church, Thomas climbed the low bank to the graveyard. There, crouched on the uneven ground of the plague dead, he could see the hunched figure of his wife, her shoulders shuddering with despairing grief. In front of her was a grey stone, hung with a garland of silk flowers, this was the grave of their precious eight-year-old daughter Jane. She had been one of the thousands of victims that had succumbed to the plague the previous year, leaving them childless and bereft. Thomas knelt down beside his wife, his lips moving in silent prayer. After some time he moved as if to lead his wife away, but she pushed him forcefully aside and sobbed more loudly. It had been like this since the day that their treasured daughter had died, and there seemed to be nothing Thomas could do to revive Elizabeth's mental state. Finally rising he stood head bowed for another minute, before turning and walking slowly away.

A quarter of a mile eastwards towards the Tower in Seething Lane, stood a large rambling building known as the Naval Office. The structure was divided into five substantial residencies with office accommodation. The area was completed by a courtyard and communal garden, with security being provided by an entry gate that was locked at night by the resident porter. In one of the residencies, a short dark energetic figure wearing a periwig hunched diligently over his desk, this was the Clerk of the Acts and his name was Samuel Pepys. The Pepys household in the mornings was a lively one, as both Samuel, and his resident clerks and house staff, made it a habit to rise early and get productive. His chief clerk was young William Hewer, a nephew of a friend, who had proved himself a great asset in assisting Pepys in his naval duties. There was also Tom Edwards who had been a chorister at the Royal Chapel until his voice broke. He had been well known to Pepys and shared his love of music, consequently he was invited into the Pepy's household to work both in the house and at the Navy Office. His team of four housemaids were headed up by Jane Birch who had worked for him from the age of fourteen. Last but not least in the residential makeup of the house was Pepys attractive wife Elizabeth, with whom he enjoyed and suffered a tempestuous, jealousy driven, love-hate relationship. The marriage had survived the eleven years in which Pepy's career and wealth had grown considerably. And now after the early years of austerity and strife, they were reaping the benefits of Samuel's lofty connections and ambitious energetic competence. In many ways the staff they surrounded themselves with substituted for the family they were unable to produce, owing to the damage Pepys suffered in an operation for the 'Stone' some years earlier.

The house had come with the job, and to Pepys, the residence was the outward sign of his progress, so not only was it clean, orderly and comfortable, but also elegantly laid out. Luxuriously decorated, and extravagantly appointed, the house was rarely free of joiners, plasterers, and painters, as Pepys constantly made alterations to his prized possession. Pepys rose from his desk and handed William Hewer some naval documents, before leaving the office to attend the twice weekly meeting with the other members of the Navy Board. Stepping out into the warm morning sunshine, Pepys walked briskly across the gated courtyard to the residence of Sir William Batten. Looking to his right he noticed that the gates were still locked, and that the porter was trying to placate a small crowd of women demanding to be heard. Pepys had some sympathy for the women, as their husbands were sailors, and they had not been paid by the navy in several months. Pepys knew the Crown's financial problems only too well, as the members of Parliament were unwilling to pour more money into the Civil List while King Charles II continued his willful extravagance. The wave of euphoria that had greeted the King's triumphal restoration six years earlier had long since faded, and now Pepys and the Navy Board had to wrestle with the ongoing financial problems on a daily basis. After being shown into the house by a housemaid, Pepys was greeted by Sir William Batten, who then proceeded to lead Pepys to the familiar long oak table where all their meetings were held. Already seated was another member of the board, Sir William Penn, Pepys exchanged greetings and sat down. Pepys could on occasion enjoy the company of these men in a social setting, but underneath the surface there existed an ongoing tension. This was caused mainly by Pepys naked ambition, and what he saw as their lack of professionalism. They in turn were rendered insecure, both by Pepys intensity in his work, and his good relationships within the higher echelons of the establishment. As per usual the Navy Boards finances was the subject to be discussed, and Pepys in his usual fashion, laid out the situation with good reason and a mastery of the facts.

In the discussion Pepys stressed that financial stringency and better allocation of the funds available was the only way forward. Penn and

Batten shifted uncomfortably in their seats, for they had benefited bounteously in the more loose culture where there was less scrutiny and attention to detail. In the many long term contracts with suppliers of ship building material, both men had excepted bribes and gifts to keep these cosy arrangements going, regardless of quality or value for money. Pepys was also prepared to accept these profitable sidelines, but not at the expense of the Crown and the Navy. The two men reluctantly agreed with Pepys that every contract should be reviewed, with the emphasis on quality of product and competitive pricing. They then agreed that they should leave for Whitehall immediately, in order to report to their immediate superior Sir George Carteret. Before leaving the Naval Office, Pepys changed into a coat decorated with gold brocade. For clothes and a smart appearance were important to him, befitting a man with rising fortunes, and who was now mixing with royalty on a regular basis. After preening himself in front of his expensive mirror glass, his fleshy facial features exhibited a self satisfied grin, and then he was away to business. After meeting Penn and Batten in the courtyard, the porter thought it best to guide Pepys and the fellow members of the Naval Office out through a side exit, in order to avoid the disgruntled crowd at the front gates. Walking briskly, the three men wasted no time as they crossed Tower Street and entered the narrow thouroughfare of Beer Lane. As they neared the Galley Quay on the Thames, they held tightly on to their hats as the warm easterly breeze blew stronger. The official Naval Office lighter was waiting to transport them upriver, and they were soon scudding away from the bank, threading a course through the multitude of river craft.

After returning from the church, Thomas Farriner helped his apprentices in the bakehouse, gathering the freshly cooked loaves and taking them along the narrow passage leading to his small shop. Saturday was the day when all receipts, payments, wages and bills, had to be settled. After returning to his shop Farriner studied his accounts and noticed, as was normally the case, that the Naval Office was behind with its payment for the King's biscuit. Shaking his head ruefully, Farriner rose from the table and departed from the shop, carrying his account book with him. It was his usual routine on a Saturday to visit the inns and taverns that he supplied in order to settle the accounts. Walking through the narrow lanes, the garrets of the facing houses above him almost touched, allowing only small chinks of daylight to filter through. Farriner noticed that the fierce summer drought had caused the timber cladding to peel away from the house walls, like the bark on a dead tree.

Turning into Thames Street, Farriner made his way through the bustle and clamour of one of the great commercial arteries of the city. This narrow street by the river was the pivotal lifeblood of London, the import and export centre of all the goods and produce of England and the trading world. Turning right into Soper Lane, he laboured uphill in the heat towards Cheapside, glancing occasionally at the houses of the soap makers that gave the lane its name. London in 1666 was prosperous, the population had increased by another 100,000 from the days of Shakespeare, and the city was expanding with its burgeoning commercial success. Once in Cheapside, Farriner made his way through the crowds to the conduit where water vendors and private citizens had congregated to draw water and exchange gossip.

After refreshing himself, he browsed the fashionable shops displaying their goods on counters open to the street. He entered one establishment that had a lavish and gilded interior lit by candles in silver holders. Looking at the silks and fine fabrics on display, Farriner decided to purchase a lace scarf for his wife, for even though all affection for him had seemed to be destroyed by her grief, he was forever hopeful that the Elizabeth he had known and cherished would return.

Reaching the end of Cheapside, Farriner passed the magnificent structure of St Paul's Cathedral on his way to the stench and filth of the River Fleet. It was hear he settled an account with his lard supplier, who resided in a squalid tavern in Seacoal Lane. Making his way back to St Paul's, he settled a number of accounts with taverns in the area of Newgate Street, where the butchers and their apprentices peddled their trade. It was an area that was particularly busy, as the massed crowds waited hungrily for their freshly killed meat. As Farriner entered St Paul's Churchyard he was feeling hot and uncomfortable, the air beneath the ever-present pall of smoke over the city was hazed with heat and dust. He decided to enter the Cathedral to get some respite from the oppressive conditions. Enjoying the coolness offered by the flagtones and massive stone pillars, he walked the length of the nave among the strolling crowds, scanning the crude stalls full of cheap mementoes. He decided to sit for a while in one of the pews, bowing his head in prayer. He silently prayed for happier days when Elizabeth would be smiling, and they would laugh together again. When he rose, he approached a marble font and splashed his face with the holy water, then stepped out again into the stifling heat of the day.

Pepys, Batten and Penn held on tightly as the lighter man rowed their boat through one of the arches of London Bridge. Coming out the other side, the lighter speeded up alarmingly as they dodged across the water crowded with river craft. As the boat settled down and continued its journey upstream, Pepys looked up from the brown smelly water of the Thames and fixed his gaze upon his two older friends. He was aware of their unease about the agreed course of action, and more importantly he knew why they were uneasy. He also wondered why he was secretly enjoying their discomfort. If he was truly honest with himself, it was because he was jealous of their distinguished naval careers. They had something that he could never hope to match, for he was not the sort of man who could have commanded a ship, or fought sea battles like them.

So to compensate for this he determined to make himself a much superior administrator. Someone who made it his business to learn everything that he needed to know, in order to gain total control. As a consequence of this diligence he had now become an authority on timber measurement, rope manufacture, sea charts, tide tables, flag-making and ship building. He prided himself on his orderliness and the importance of getting the details right, his insistence on keeping the written records of both officers and ships proved invaluable when he wanted to prove a point. Born the son of a tailor in Fleet Street, he had been fortunate in having distant relatives of a higher standing. These relations were prepared to give a helping hand to an intelligent, energetic young man, in terms of both education and career. One of these relations was Lord Sandwich, someone who, like Batten and Penn, had been a prominent part of the late Oliver Cromwell's power base. These men were in a position of considerable influence, and ready to offer valuable expertise to the newly restored King when they thought the time was right to do so. The young, ambitious, social climber Pepys, had benefited hugely from Lord Sandwich's skilful manoeuverings between the two regimes, and Pepys in turn, had made sure he took full advantage.

On being appointed to the Naval Office, Pepys soon realised that the administration practices were totally inadequate in handling the Government funds in a controlled way. As a consequence massive debt and corrupt practices were rife throughout the system. Though he enjoyed the prosperous social life that men like Penn and Batten entertainingly offered, he was at the same time appalled by their complacency. Their apparent willingness to take the benefits of office without putting in the professional effort, went totally against Pepys principals. Pepys was brought back from his mental musings by the lighter suddenly bumping against the Whitehall Palace boat-stairs. It was called a Palace but in reality it was nothing more than a vast jumble of houses with the great Banqueting Hall rising behind them. The three men alighted from the boat and made their way to the office of Sir George Carteret, treasurer to the Navy Board and in effect the boss of Pepys, Penn and Batten.

Being a friend of Lord Sandwich, Carteret was well disposed to Pepys, and Pepys in turn knew he had to cultivate him. Sitting around the table, Pepys immediately took it upon himself to explain in impressive detail the reason for their visit. Only occasionally did he have to argue away the mild protests of Penn and Batten, and with the promise of more quality for less money, Carteret was won over. They rose from the table and headed for the King's Closet in the chapel. After speaking to the courtiers there, they were escorted up the Privy Stairs to the first floor, before entering the long gallery hung with paintings and rich tapestries. On entering the Presence Chamber, Pepys could not help but feel invigorated, for he responded to anything that was picturesque. With its lavish French furniture, and velvet-lined musical instruments ornamented with silver gilt, it was the ultimate in elaborate splendour. Only the select few were permitted to pass beyond the Presence Chamber into the Privy Chamber, and there waiting to receive them was the tall dark figure of the King. Though Pepys loved the grandeur and trappings of Royal Power, his opinion of the King was ambiguous. He welcomed the King's patronage of the theatre, painting and music, plus his whimsical interest in the sciences, which were all great passions of Pepys. But in Pepys eyes Charles II threw away his advantages by not taking his kingly role seriously enough, preferring amusement and pleasure to hard work, dignity and glory. Clever but easily bored, the King appeared to lack both mental stamina and depth of character.

The four members of the Navy Board bowed graciously to the King, before Carteret and Pepys outlined their proposals in subservient fashion. The King nodded approvingly as the details poured forth. He particularly appreciated the detailed knowledge, competence and work ethic displayed by Pepys, shrewdly recognizing that here was a man whose obvious hunger for position and wealth, could be turned to the Crowns advantage. With the King giving his complete support to the strategy, he suddenly picked up some exotic caged birds, dismissed the members of the Navy Board with a wave of the Royal hand, and retired to the Withdrawing Room. On leaving the Palace, Penn and Batten returned to the Boatman waiting at the boat-stairs to be taken back to the Navy Office. Meanwhile Pepys had bid his friends farewell as he had some important business at the Royal Exchange. Provided with a Hackney Coach, Pepys made himself comfortable as he was transported from west to east, stopping and starting through the crowded narrow streets. Pepys felt satisfied that the morning had gone well, but he realised he would have to deliver real benefits, and it was for this reason he was making his way to the Royal Exchange.

It was early afternoon and Thomas Farriner had almost finished his round of account settling. The collection had been more uncomfortable and tiring than was usual because of the heat and windblown dust, and he was in need of some refreshment. He stepped into a small tavern in Eastcheap that was the last account to be settled. Agreeing with the landlord that a free meal could be his payment, he ordered some mutton, with venison pasty, served with bread and a small beer. He ate quietly in the corner looking out into the street. Because it was Saturday when all accounts were settled, all establishments would be staying open till late, accommodating those with money to spend.

Samuel Pepys alighted himself from the carriage at the Royal Exchange and gave the coachman two silver shillings. As the carriage pulled away, Pepys turned to face the Exchange that was widely recognised as the cathedral of commerce. The double-arched entrance led into the vast quadrangle surrounded by a marble-pillared colonnade, a bell tower rose above the arched entrance with a huge clock set in its southern face. As Pepys entered the large inner courtyard, he was reminded once again of why his work was so important to him, and why it gave him so much pleasure. For along with the self-discipline and self-worth, it gave him wealth, public esteem, and life enhancing experience.

The area opening up in front of Pepys was swarming with merchants bearing news before buying and selling, with some merchants still settling their weekly accounts. Above them on the two circular balconied galleries, nobles, gallants and fine ladies strolled past shops where all the luxuries of the known world were assembled. It was here that Pepys hoped to negotiate superior contracts for the Navy in timber, hemp, tar, canvas, resin and nails. By using the large network of merchants he had courted before the days developments, he was now confident that deals could be struck. He knew that he was going to make many enemies among the existing suppliers, not to mention Penn and Batten. His two eminent colleagues had been involved in the cosy long-standing arrangements that had been formed through the profligate years. Those years of paying exorbitant prices for inferior products, had proved damaging to the quality of ship production, and resulted in shameful funding shortages when paying the seamen. Pepys felt that it was his professional and patriotic duty to raise the navy's prestige and build the sailors morale. Consequently, he was more than prepared to accept the inevitable character assassination and backstabbing that would result in pursuing that noble cause.

Samuel Pepys leaned against one of the marble pillars, enjoying the coolness and respite from the heat of the day, his eyes keenly scanning the chattering merchants indulging in their business. A tall smartly dressed figure broke away from the crowd and approached Pepys, they greeted each other warmly, knowing that the business they were about to discuss could be mutually beneficial. They retreated to a small eating house on one of the raised galleries, where they ordered a small snack of bread and cheese washed down with a dry white sack wine imported from Spain. The tall man handed over a handsome silver coin worth a half-crown to the proprietor, and led Pepys to a corner table.

Pepy's companion was the biggest timber merchant in southern England and had yards in Essex, Rotherhithe, and Wapping. His name was William Warren and he had targeted Pepys some weeks earlier, knowing that Pepys had influence in the Navy Board. Two weeks previously Warren had taken Pepys down to Wapping to explain the timber industry to him. Pepys was a willing pupil as he listened with intelligence and interest, knowing that such knowledge was power. By the end of the lesson Pepys was fully versed in how the cutting and sawing of timber was so important to the quality of the final product. The next day Pepys had visited the yard of the existing longstanding supplier William Wood. Armed with his newly acquired knowledge, Pepys examined the work practices and soon recognised the inferior timbers being produced and the reasons why. Back at the Navy Office Pepys had studied the accounts of William Wood, deducing immediately that Sir William Batten had benefited hugely in the association, much to the detriment of the Navy.

Now at the Royal Exchange Pepys was finally in a position to smash that cosy cartel, as he told Warren that the massive navy timber contract was his for the asking. The two men shook hands and finished their wine, but as Pepys rose from the table Warren gave him a pair of gloves and put his finger to his lips. Pepys slightly curious, put them carefully into his coat pocket and said his goodbyes. Finding a quiet corner, Pepys retrieved the gloves to find they contained 40 gold pieces. Pepys, hardly able to contain his excitement, could not have been happier with the days business. As Clerk of the Acts he had often been a recipient of gifts, and if he was honest, small bribes, it was an accepted benefit of the position, but this bounty had been of a much higher order. He had formed a contract with a supplier who offered a better product for less money, while at the same time being lucratively rewarded on a personal level. With more contracts to be formalised, he realised with barely suppressed euphoria, that at the still young age of 33, his expanding wealth was set to go even higher. Feeling exhilarated, Pepys turned eastwards and walked towards his house in Seething Lane, he had promised to take his wife Elizabeth on a picnic trip up the Thames to Greenwich Park that afternoon.

Thomas Farriner finally left the small tavern in Eastcheap to make his way back to Pudding Lane. Holding the lace scarf he had purchased for Elizabeth, he still had hopes that his gift would bring back a glimmer of light and affection to her eyes. Just before turning into the lane he saw a familiar figure walking briskly, while unmistakably displaying an air of self importance. Samuel Pepys was an easily recognisable figure to Thomas Farriner on the streets of London. Always walking swiftly, his periwig gave him an enduring image as he made his way to and fro between the Naval Office and his daily business. Thomas saw the opportunity to inquire about the late payments from the Naval Office and the settling of his accounts. Addressing him politely as Mr Pepys, Thomas stopped Pepys in his tracks and introduced himself as Thomas Farriner the King's Baker. Though Pepys did not recognise the man appearing before him, he was familiar with the name, as he had seen it many times on his balance sheet for victuals. Though he was in a hurry Pepys was in a good mood; his encounter at the Royal Exchange had given him an extra skip in his step.

As a representative of both the Crown and the Navy he felt responsible for the late payments, while also knowing Farriner had proved a good supplier of the ship's biscuit. As Farriner expressed his grievance, Pepys pulled out one of his gold coins and gave it to Farriner, telling him it could go to his account. Pepys then walked on hurriedly, taking care to keep close to the wall under the shelter of the jetties, in order to avoid the swill that was occasionally emptied from the upstairs windows.

Farriner was left staring incredulously at the glinting gold coin in his hand, suddenly aware of possible thieves, he thrust it deeply into his pockets and hurried towards Pudding Lane. Once inside his house he excitedly called out for his wife, but the house was eerily silent. He ran from room to room, but there was no sign of Elizabeth. She had disappeared before, sometimes for days, usually she went to stay at her sister's place in Southwark. Suddenly overcome with deep melancholy, he dropped the lace scarf wearily on the floor and began to weep silently. He knew that the problem with Elizabeth was that she partly blamed him for the loss of Jane. His failure to move the family away from London when the plague first erupted, was a constant source of torment for both of them. But the truth was that this would have been impossible, as his business and the families very livelihood depended on residing in the capital. After sometime he reached for the scarf and placed it on the table beside a plate of uneaten boiled beef. Sighing deeply, he retreated to his bedroom and carefully put Pepys gold coin in his strongbox under the bed. He then left to check the apprentices in the bakehouse and pay their wages.

Samuel Pepys made his way briskly through the gates of the Naval Office and into the courtyard. Entering the house he saw his maid Jane preparing a picnic basket, he playfully pinched an apple before entering his chambers to wash and change. On entering his study he approached some glass-fronted bookcases of which he was extremely proud, they had been purpose built by a naval joiner, and were the perfect setting for his ever-growing collection of books. He reached up to one of the shelves and brought down a simulated book made of wood, it had been hollowed out inside to make a recess. He then proceeded to place the remaining 39 gold pieces inside the book and returned it to the shelf. He finally emerged from his chambers wearing a white silk shirt with cream breeches, buckle boots and a black wide brimmed hat.

He cheerfully presented himself to his wife who was standing ready to leave with Jane and house assistant Tom Edwards. On the short walk to the boatman at Galley Quay Pepys was in high spirits, tapping his bamboo walking stick on the ground as he joyfully sang his favourite theatre songs. Elizabeth and Jane joined in with the singing as Tom Edwards, laden with the picnic box, struggled to keep up with them. They headed eastwards upriver into a stiffening warm breeze, with everyone having to hang on to their hats, before alighting at Greenwich Pier. The happy party were still singing as they stopped halfway up the hill, after finding a suitable picnic spot. Jane opened the picnic box to reveal a variety of foodstuffs, including cold turkey pie, a barrel of oysters, bread and butter, and some bottles of wine embossed with Pepys personal crest.

Throughout the feasting, Pepys continued to display high spirits, showing considerable goodwill to Elizabeth and the company in general. At one stage Pepys walked up towards the top of the hill near the castle. Elizabeth watched him wistfully, their volatile relationship could at times be exhausting, so she cherished these precious moments of peace and tranquility. As Pepys sat down at the top of the hill looking backwards across the loops of the river towards London's spires and smoke, he thought back to his early days of financial struggle. Comparing them to his present bountiful circumstances, he had to concede that on the issue of money he was undoubtedly greedy but not miserly, for his appetite for life was too voracious to neglect the benefits that lucrative wealth could bring. The public esteem associated with the position of Clerk of the Acts also opened doors to other interesting outlets, as his recent election to the Royal Society so satisfyingly demonstrated. Though his own scientific credentials were almost non-existent, his intellectual liveliness and curiosity was greatly stimulated by discussions with great original minds like Hooke, Boyle, and Wren.

Thinking back to his encounter with the King's Baker earlier that day, it gave him great satisfaction that he was in a position to renumerate him on behalf of the Navy. Pepys saw it as further confirmation of his success and growing influence. He was brought out of his thoughts by Elizabeth encouraging him to join in a game of catch ball, reluctantly he dragged himself to his feet and made his way down the hill.

Thomas Farriner, as was customary on settlement Saturday, had paid his apprentices their wages and had joined them on their usual late afternoon visit to the King's Head Tavern in nearby Fish Street Hill. It was on Saturdays that Thomas missed his previous family life the most. It had been their favourite day together when they could relax with their daughter Jane at the end of the week, playing cards and chess, and laughing in each others company. Sadly those treasured days were now gone forever. He found it easier to forget in the crowded congenial atmosphere of the Tavern, smoking his pipe, supping his beer, and watching the players at the dice and shovel-board tables.

Aided by the strong following wind, the Thames waterman made swift progress as he rowed Pepys and the rest of the picnic party back to Galley Quay. As they alighted they heard the hungry echoing roars of the lions that were held captive in the White Tower of London. They were kept as a leisure attraction in the menagerie, and Pepys never tired of viewing them when time permitted. They listened for a moment before walking uphill in the direction of Seething Lane.

Thomas Farriner smiled benignly as he sat in the corner of the tavern, his apprentices had already left and he was beginning to lose all track of time. The beer he had copiously drunk had frozen the moment, and he was now in a state of comfortable numbness, his usual condition come Saturday evenings. As darkness fell it was his regular routine to visit the various inns and taverns that lined the street on the short walk back to his home. It was always the same order, The Hoop, followed by The Star, then the Mitre, finishing up with the Golden Cup. After rising slowly from his table, Farriner shuffled unsteadily out of the establishment, and into the gathering gloom of the evening.

Samuel Pepys could hear the sound of laughter and cheerful singing coming from the music room, he was eager to join in the fun and show off his Viola playing, but first he had an important duty to perform. Sitting at the desk in his office he held a fat paper-covered notebook in his hand, he opened it to reveal white pages with neat margins lined in red ink down the left-hand side of each page. He then proceeded to write in a neat shorthand his personal account of the days events, for this was a diary he had kept for the last six years, a self-imposed duty that he undertook with due seriousness. Eventually rising with a grunt of satisfaction, he placed the diary carefully in his desk-drawer before leaving the office to join the company in the music room.

Thomas Farriner rose shakily from his seat, and lurching from side to side, his brain scrambled by alcohol, made his way out of the Golden Cup Tavern. Inside the Tavern there had been the warm smell of ale and tobacco, the glow of candle-light, and the buzz of human talk and laughter. Once outside there was enveloping darkness, and a strong high wind. Entering the inky blackness of Pudding Lane, he frequently found himself bumping into disused chamber pots, sacks of rubbish and discarded broken furniture. The wind above him whistled around the chimney stacks and gables, causing a loose slate to slide down a roof and shatter on the cobbles nearby. Nearing his house, Thomas crossed a tiny yard and went into the bakehouse. Inside the walls were blackened by soot, a grey coating of flour and dust coloured the floor and work surfaces, giving a ghostly illumination in the shadowy gloom. After picking up an unlit candle, Thomas raked up some dying embers in the oven, creating just enough flame to light his wick. After slowly tottering across the yard, he noticed the back door of the house swinging open on its hinges.

He assumed that Elizabeth had returned and had failed to lock up, but on entering the house, all was dark and silent. As he swayed unsteadily past the scullery table, he failed to notice that the boiled beef and lace scarf had been removed. After climbing the narrow stairs and satisfying himself that the house was empty, he entered his own chamber. After extinguishing the candle and collapsing on the bed, deep slumber came immediately.

Samuel Pepys climbed into his impressive four-poster bed, still singing his favourite songs and playfully teasing his wife Elizabeth as regards her musical abilities with the Viola. He had learnt to play the instrument as a boy in his schooldays at St Paul's, and he had been giving some basic lessons to Elizabeth in recent weeks. The musical evening had been a great success, with much singing and dancing, complimented with good wine and foodstuffs. Pepys had again took the opportunity to show his musical prowess to the assembled guests, and for him it had been the perfect end to a highly satisfying day. With a dinner party scheduled for the following day Pepys realised he must get some sleep, so within seconds of bidding Elizabeth goodnight Pepys was snoring obliviously.

In the graveyard of St Margeret's, Elizabeth Farriner crouched beside her daughter's grave. Holding the lace scarf to her cheek, she was perfectly still and deep in thought.

It was the place in which she had spent the vast majority of her waking hours, ever since the shattering tragedy that had befallen them. Even though it was well past midnight, she felt perfectly secure among the plague dead, the evening was warm and her beloved daughter lay close by. Suddenly for the first time since Jane's death, she was thinking of her life before her daughter was born, in particular her life with Thomas.

In the early evening she had returned from visiting her sister, and had seen the lace scarf on the table. She knew that it was yet another gift from Thomas, one of many that he had bestowed on her in recent months. Up to now she had been impervious to these overtures, being far too absorbed in her anguish, but curiously this time she had been deeply moved. Standing in the silent empty house, she had suddenly felt tenderness for her husband for the first time in months. Initially she had felt confused by these feelings, and had left the house preoccupied and distracted, forgetting to close the door behind her. Holding the scarf to her face, she had made her way to the graveyard, and had remained there throughout the night. Like the sun breaking behind a cloud, she now realised with stunning clarity, how cruel and unfair she had been to Thomas. She now remembered how happy he had made her feel before their loss. Abruptly rising from the grave, she resolved to tell him immediately how sorry she was, and that they would and could be happy again. Running through the narrow alley down to the bakery, she was vaguely aware of a crackling noise that seemed to get louder as she neared Pudding Lane. As she turned into the yard of the bakery, her expression turned to one of acute terror.

In the early hours of the morning, somewhere between one and two o'clock, Thomas Farriner awoke with a start. He had been dreaming of Elizabeth, she had been calling to him, it had seemed so very real. But now all he could hear was the whistle of the wind, and a vague cracking of timbers. Then Elizabeth's voice came again, she was shouting somewhere nearby. His senses clearing, Thomas felt a choking sensation, it was then he realised the room was full of smoke.

He leaped from the bed and groped his way to the window, throwing it wide open he inhaled deeply, before running to the door. Once outside he found the corridor filled with smoke, Thomas immediately dropped to his knees and crawled towards his daughter's old room. As he did so he heard the crackle of fire, and saw the flames on the stairs climbing fast towards the upper floors. On entering the room, he rushed across to the window and thrust his head and shoulders outside. Staring desperately down into the yard, he could just make out the figure of Elizabeth, her arms outstretched, beside herself with horror. There was a sheer drop of 20ft into the yard, but Thomas, seeing some bags of flour, shouted to Elizabeth to stack them below the window. Composing herself quickly, she stacked them three deep in order to cushion the fall. It was at this point that Thomas remembered the strongbox under his bed. Turning back towards the corridor, Thomas could only see thick black smoke and feel the heat of the blazing staircase. Hesitating for a second, he could see that it was now impossible to get back to his room and survive. Reluctantly he turned back towards the window and jumped into Elizabeth's arms, their future now firmly in the hands of God.

To the east in Seething Lane, Jane Birch rose early from her bed. Though it was still only 3 o'clock in the morning, she realised that the preparations for the dinner party scheduled that day, needed to be set in motion as soon as possible. Her bedroom was positioned high in the Garret of Samuel Pepy's residence in the Naval Office. Turning towards the window that faced westwards, she saw a golden glow of fire illuminating the sky in the vicinity of London Bridge. After getting dressed quickly, she ran excitedly downstairs to wake the master of the house. A disgruntled Pepys, greatly put out by being awoken from a deep sleep, put on his gown and opened the door. On being told of the fire he accompanied Jane up to her Garret-Room, grumbling all the time that fires in London were not uncommon as he climbed the stairs. On viewing the fire from the Garret, Pepys decided that the flames were not near enough to be a threat. He then turned to Jane and assured her confidently that the fire would probably blow itself out overnight, before descending the winding stairs to his bedroom.

4

LONDON
APRIL 1755

The early morning skies over London dawned grey and cloudy, as a persistent band of heavy rain drenched the awakening city streets. The roofs of the mediaeval houses that overhung Fleet Street created rivulets of water that poured down onto the guttered streets below, making a foul slippery mix of horse manure, straw and mud. Besides the dominant industries of publishing, book-selling and printing, the Fleet Street neighbourhood was a vibrant mix of coffee houses, taverns, chop houses, gin shops, wig-makers, and snuff dealers. This part of the city had narrowly escaped the ravages of the Great Fire in 1666, so much of the structure had remained as it appeared the previous century.

In the winding alleys to the north behind Fleet Street, amid a tangle of narrow lanes and dark alleys in a quiet L shaped court, stood Number 17 Gough Square. Built at the end of the 17th century, the town house had three main storeys, with a large attic room at the top, and some fine bay windows overlooking the square. The house that morning was a hive of activity and industry, with servants and residents regularly negotiating the tall central staircase. The hub of this activity seemed to be centered around the attic room, with people entering and departing carrying books and sheaves of paper. Each entry and exit seemed to be accompanied by a loud booming voice from inside, which reverberated through the house.

Inside the room the floor was covered with hundreds of books, slips of paper, and notebooks, with half-filled boxes and half-eaten meals completing the scene of organized chaos. There were three men in the room, of which two were frantically writing down notes from the mass of books in front of them. The third man, talking loudly, was sitting at a desk facing a large bay window. He was leaning intently over his writing paper, occasionally barking out orders to the two men in an abrupt and forthright manner, giving the impression of the utmost urgency. Suddenly with a roar of exultation, he rose from his desk and turned towards the two men. Blotting out the weak daylight from the bay-window behind him, he was at that moment a rare sight to behold. Uncommonly tall at six feet, stout and stooped, he carried himself with an awkward demeanour, full of involuntary tics and movements. His forehead and ill-fitting frizzy wig bore scorch marks, caused by reading too close to lighted candles and oil lamps. His generous features were pock-marked, legacies of childhood illnesses, and his mouth habitually opened and shut as if chewing something. He was dressed in a dirty brown coat and breeches, his shirt collar and sleeves were unbuttoned, and his stockings were down to his feet. Along with the two other men he had worked diligently through the night, and now their task was done. His name was Samuel Johnson, and after nine burdensome years his Dictionary was complete.

David Garrick stirred in his bed. The previous night had been a long one, and the memory of it made him reluctant to face the day ahead. His German wife Eva, had already risen and was talking with the servants downstairs. The discussion was all about the headlines in the morning news sheets, and in particular, the previous evening's events at the Drury Lane Theatre. Exasperated by late arrivals at his theatre performances, David Garrick had proposed to abolish half price seats for those who entered his theatre after the third act. This had provoked a mini riot half way through the previous evenings performance, with fights breaking out between the players and the spectators. As a result of the violence, some considerable damage had been inflicted to the Theatre in both the pit and the galleries.

Violence was not uncommon in theatres, but the bad publicity contained in the morning new sheets was something Garrick could well have done without. The fact that it was his new price initiative that provoked the riot was an added irritant. Eventually joining his wife for breakfast, Garrick was not his usual lighthearted self, his head was slightly aching and the headlines in the news sheets did not promote much comfort. He had been married to his wife and soulmate Eva for six years. She did her best to raise his spirits, as she reminded him that it was a rare reversal to his usual good fortune. Garrick looked at his attractive wife and had to agree, his life over the last ten years had been charmed and positively glowing in personal success. Eighteen years after traveling down to London in the company of his friend and tutor Samuel Johnson – both from the town of Lichfield in Staffordshire – he had achieved a notoriety and lifestyle way beyond anything he could possibly have imagined.

Eight years younger than his Lichfield traveling companion, Garrick had originally arrived in London to be trained in the legal profession for a career in the Temple. Quickly realising that the law courts were not for him, he decided to indulge his enthusiasm for live theatre. Short of stature but handsome of feature, his vivacious personality and natural ability to perform both comedy and tragedy, swiftly elevated him to one of the leading actors in the country. His drawing power at the box office became enormous, mainly at the Theatre Royal in Drury Lane, which he had made his theatrical home since debuting there in 1742. In the spring of 1747 he was wealthy enough to be able to purchase a half interest in Drury Lane for £12000, thereby catapulting himself into the world of theatrical management and enhancing his powers on the stage. The world of theatre had also brought him a loving wife, having met Eva when she was a dancer with a German Opera chorus group.

As he looked around him at the fine tapestries and rich gilded interior of his smart London townhouse, his spirits began to return to their usual levels – he had much to be thankful for.

Back at number 17 Gough Square Samuel Johnson and his two assistants sat drinking copious cups of tea. The realisation that their task was complete was slowly sinking in, and though they were exhausted through lack of sleep, their feeling of achievement would have made slumber impossible. The two men with Johnson were linguist Victor Peyton, and experienced reference worker Alexander Macbean. Both men were the type of needy souls that Johnson would habitually help assist, by way of bed and board plus financial support. It was one of the reasons that Samuel Johnson was never financially stable for very long. A combination of sympathy for the struggling underdog, and a desperate, sometimes morbid fear of being alone, contributed to his income never matching his outgoings. Eventually both Peyton and Macbean retreated from the attic room, leaving Johnson alone with his thoughts. He was finding it difficult to absorb the reality that after nine long years, his Dictionary project had finally been completed. After arriving in London with his former pupil David Garrick at the age of 27, his attempts to launch a profitable literary career had been littered with false starts and cruel disappointments. He was becoming known in the Fleet Street environs as someone who was touched by genius, but unable to produce a defining literary classic. The concept of the Dictionary had been proposed at a time when his literary lifestyle was rewarding him very little for huge amounts of work. At the advancing age of 37, Johnson felt at that time, the Dictionary could provide a lifeline for his literary reputation and financial security.

His friend Robert Dodsley, a successful bookseller, had approached Johnson at his digs in Holburn, convincing him that he had the encyclopedic cast of mind to satisfy the dire need Britain had for a Dictionary. Johnson had certainly been aware that there was no comprehensive listing of the English language, and in his more ambitious moments had contemplated the idea. But on each occasion he had dismissed the notion, feeling it was far too bold and large a project. Before coming to London he had run a school in Lichfield with his wife Tetty. She was 20 years his senior and the relationship had never been an easy one. Eventually joining him in London, she had not adapted well either to the city, or the insecure lifestyle of a writer struggling to get recognition and financial security. Desperately unhappy she had slipped into a life of drink and opium dependency, and Johnson feeling partly responsible, felt the Dictionary was a way to improve their lives.

Dodsley had explained to him that the Dictionary was to be backed by an impressive syndicate of successful booksellers, all great admirers of Johnson. After a meeting with the six-man syndicate at the Golden Anchor Tavern near Holborn Bar, Johnson had been impressive enough to convince them they were on to a good thing. Shaking hands on the deal, they agreed to pay him £1,575 to be paid in installments over three years. At that time it was his first substantial payment for literary labour of any kind. It would have been a large enough contract for any author, and almost immediately it enabled him and his wife to move into Gough Square. Johnson, now sitting alone in his attic, was suddenly overwhelmed with sorrow. The Dictionary was now completed but his wife Tetty had died three years earlier. The move to Gough Square had tragically failed to halt her downward spiral, and Johnson had been filled with both guilt and regret.

The melancholy and depression triggered after her death had slowed Johnson in his work, with the Dictionary now being completed six years later than the original estimate. As Johnson sat staring out of the rain soaked bay window, almost in a trance, his pet cat Hodge leapt on to his lap and snapped him back to consciousness. Rising from the desk he picked up the last proofed sheet of the Dictionary, looked at it ruefully, then proceeded to descend the long staircase to his bedroom. He emerged from the room wearing a snuff colour coat with gold buttons, complimented by black worsted stockings. His overall look was one of shabby genteel, with sartorial elegance never being his strong point. He called out to a young Negro boy who was a servant in the house, his name was Frank Barber and he had been a former slave in Jamaica. Again displaying his empathy for the downtrodden, Johnson had taken him under his wing on the recommendation of a friend. Handing Frank the last proofed sheet, Johnson instructed him to take it to the print office of his good friend William Strahan, who lived nearby in Little New Street. Andrew Millar, a member of the six-man syndicate, was also at the print office. He was there waiting to receive the concluding sheet, having arranged to meet Johnson for that lunchtime in the nearby Cheshire Cheese Tavern in Fleet Street.

Meanwhile just short of a mile to the west, David Garrick slipped on his expensive woollen coat, embroidered with metal braid at the front edges. The garment was worn open at the front to display his brightly embossed waistcoat, an expensive pair of shoes with diamond cut buckles completed his apparel. Leaving his wife Eva in their Southampton Street House in Covent Garden, he quickly hailed a Sedan Chair, as the falling rain had caused much mud to be formed on the pavements. Handing the carriers a silver shilling coin, he asked to be taken to the Drury Lane Theatre just a few streets away. Garrick was hoping that the repairs to his playhouse were well underway after the previous evenings damage.

Arriving at the theatre a few minutes later, Garrick was pleased to see that the carpenters had already begun their restoration. After a short conversation with the carpenters, he was given the encouraging news that there was every likelihood of future performances being postponed for only a week. As Garrick keenly surveyed the work repairs, a highly coloured private coach enamelled in gold arrived in Drury Lane. Drawn by four excellent horses, it was driven by a richly liveried footman, it's iron wheels screeching to a halt on the granite cobbles. A smartly dressed man of senior years alighted from the carriage, and with an air of superior authority entered the playhouse. His name was James Lacey, and he was the joint owner of the Drury Lane Theatre in partnership with Garrick. The two men greeted each other warmly, though Lacey was the senior partner, he greatly recognised and appreciated the impact and influence that Garrick had brought to the theatre. They stood to one side and discussed the events of the night before. Finally agreeing they could not risk the chance of the same hostility again, they decided to accept the latecomers as an occupational cross to bear.

Samuel Johnson left his house in Gough Square, and embarked on the short walk through Wine Office Court to the Cheshire Cheese Tavern. The rain was still falling but beginning to ease, as he entered the tavern and sat at his favourite table in the chop-room. He was soon joined by Andrew Millar who congratulated him on his completion of the Dictionary. Johnson accepted the compliments with diplomatic restraint, for in the nine year duration of the project there had been understandable friction between Johnson and some of the syndicate members. The six year delay had at times caused arguments, despair and frustration, with Millar being one of Johnson's most open critics. But now over a mug of beer all was forgiven, with the relieved joint realisation they had come to a culmination in their contract.

The two men fell silent as they feasted on buttock of Beef and leg of Pork, finishing off with Plum Pudding in melted butter. Johnson was a big man with an appetite to match. Eating was one of his major pleasures, and it rarely failed to raise his spirits. Soon after finishing the meal, with Millar paying the two shillings needed to settle the bill, they were joined by Johnson's printer friend William Strahan. The three men discussed the completion of the Dictionary in some depth, before Strahan mentioned in conversation the previous evenings fracas at the Drury Lane Theatre. Samuel Johnson was interested to hear of Garrick's misadventure, the story somehow giving Johnson a further fillip to his spirit levels. His feelings toward the great thespian were complex. He felt great pride in what Garrick had achieved as a representative of their native town of Lichfield. He also retained a great fondness for 'Young Davy' as Johnson would affectionately call him. Despite this, Johnson could not help feeling envious of his former pupil, for unlike himself, Garrick seemed to have a life where most things went his way. This jealousy would manifest in Johnson's critical reviews of Garrick's plays, even though he would defend Garrick vigorously to any outside criticism. Unlike Garrick, Johnson had felt his life had been a struggle. Suffering numerous illnesses as a child, he was the son of an anxious mother and a melancholy father.

As a promising student in Oxford, his education at Pembroke College had been cut short due to lack of funds. Being physically unattractive and enduring an unhappy tragic marriage, had reinforced these negative feelings.

His failure – despite hard graft – to transform his undisputed literary genius into tangible fame and fortune, only served to highlight the contrast between Garrick and himself. On impulse Johnson decided to pay a visit to his actor friend, and resolved to walk off the meal with a vigorous stroll in the direction of Covent Garden. After further discussions on the timing of the Dictionary's publication, Johnson finally bid his farewell to Strahan and Millar outside the Tavern. As Johnson set off westwards towards the Strand, the rain had ceased to fall, and small shafts of weak sunshine were beginning to pierce through the heavy grey clouds. Johnson always preferred to walk rather than take a chair, even though there was always the chance of being the victim of a violent robbery. It was for this reason that Johnson regularly carried a heavy cudgel in his coat pocket, but he rarely had cause to use it. His sheer size and physicality often persuaded potential assailants to seek out easier prey.

After the Great Fire in 1666, the engines of wealth and power had generated the renovation of London in a rebuilding and extension to the west. The city was now the most vibrantly wealthy in the world with a population of 700,000, with one in six of the total population of England being drawn to London at some time in their lives. Samuel Johnson loved the noise of the city, it made him feel less isolated and more alive. So different to the deathly silence of the early hours in his rooms at Gough Square, where he would find his mind feeding on itself and creating inner demons of black depression. Listening to the general uproar of wagons and bells, and seeing the congregation of people of all races, talents and fortunes, going about their business, released in Johnson a massive air of expectancy and exhilaration. Johnson passed under Temple Bar, the narrow archway where Fleet Street met the Strand, doing his best to negotiate the usual build up of human traffic that afflicted this area on a daily basis.

The Strand had been redeveloped on a splendid scale, and was now as famous, and rather grander, than Cheapside in the city. Johnson perused the shop fronts curiously as he made his way through the throngs of humanity, his considerable intellect rationalising the products and novelties laid out before him. Eventually reaching Southampton Street, he turned right and headed up to Number 27 on the left hand side, the home of his good friend David Garrick. On answering the door the servant recognised the unmistakable figure of Samuel Johnson, as he had seen him before on a number of occasions. He also noticed Johnson's muddied shoes and soiled stockings, but before he could mention their condition, Eva came to the door and welcomed Johnson in. She also noticed his muddied state, but having come to know him well, knew that this hero of the English Language was eloquent of speech but careless of hygiene.

Informing Johnson that Garrick was out but expected soon, she guided him to a table laid out with a silver gilt tea service. Johnson held Eva in high esteem. He admired her elegance, femininity and cool intelligence, and welcomed this opportunity to have her full attention. After enquiring about the previous evening's fracas at the theatre, he told her of the completion of the Dictionary. She listened fascinated as he made it clear that his published Dictionary would be innovative, using extensive use of quotations drawn from the best literary sources, in order to best illustrate the meanings of words. He also confessed to her that he would be in a state of some anxiousness while he waited for publication, not knowing for certain how it will be received by the critics. As Johnson drank countless cups of tea, Eva teasingly told him that his reviews of her husband's plays would not be held against him, and that they were justly proud to know him.

Johnson momentarily felt slightly shamed, as he compared their generosity of spirit to his own mean mindedness regarding his old pupil. After some 20 minutes, David Garrick and James Lacey returned from the Theatre and joined them at the table. Garrick was always pleased to see his old friend, and after giving an account of the Drury Lane uproar, listened enthusiastically to Johnson's news of his Dictionary. Garrick had lent Johnson some books from his extensive library in order to help Johnson in his labours, but he thought it prudent not to ask for them back. Johnson's harsh treatment of books was well known, and their condition now could only be guessed at. As they talked, Johnson was reminded once again of why Garrick was hard to dislike. His open friendly countenance and warm humorous manner, were both cheering and infectious. James Lacey listened captivated as the banter between Garrick and Johnson spanned across a wide range of subjects, interspersed with much humour and wisdom.

Some years earlier Lacey had led a syndicate to purchase Ranelagh Gardens in Chelsea, consisting of a large house and spacious grounds. Lacey immediately saw the possibilities of opening it up to the richer clientele who were living to the west of the city, and so after further investment it was converted into a pleasure garden. It had proved a great success with both Londoners and tourists, adding considerably to Lacey's abundant wealth. Lacey eventually managed to find a gap in the conversation, in order to extend an invitation to the assembled company. He suggested that they ride out to the gardens in his carriage that afternoon. Ranelagh had been one of Johnson's favourite venues for some time, so never one to turn down a social invitation with company he enjoyed, he accepted graciously. Leaving the house in Southampton Street, the happy party climbed into the luxuriously appointed carriage, and set off in a westerly direction.

Looking out of the carriage window, Johnson became powerfully aware once again of the growing wealth of the capital. The swamp and marsh that had previously occupied the many areas between the city and Chelsea had long gone. The area was now immaculately laid out with wide roads and fashionable squares with gardens, surrounded by imposing four-storey houses. Johnson never tired of seeing them: Berkeley Square, Hanover Square, Grosvenor Square, all were a delight to the eyes of the passengers. Eventually leaving the built up area, they saw the vast expanse of Hyde Park stretching away to their right, before splashing their way through the marshy fields of Pimlico.

Eventually passing through the gates of Ranelagh, it was immediately noticeable that despite the lack of sunshine, the gardens were still heavily attended by the wealthy gallants with their ladies. To be admitted would have normally cost two shillings and sixpence per person, but James Lacey presented himself to the attendants and the carriage was waved through. Dismounting from the carriage, the passengers feasted their eyes on the pleasant view before them.

Ranelagh House itself stood to the north of the gardens. To the west was an ornamental lake and canal with gondolas, while among the wide variety of plants and hedges was a decoratively designed Chinese Pavilion. Even in daylight the gardens were enlightened with a thousand golden lamps, intended to emulate the effect of the noon day sun. The main feature, however, was a striking Rococo Rotunda measuring 150ft in diameter, incorporating a Central Bandstand where classical music was played, surrounded by two tiers of 52 booths. It was to this amenity that Lacey and his guests were drawn first. After settling into one of the booths and ordering sandwiches and coffee, they listened peacefully to the melodious playing of the mini orchestra.

Many people strolled around the orchestra on the matted floors that were carefully placed, in order that their footsteps should not be heard above the music. Music was not one of Johnson's great passions, but seeing the therapeutic effect it was having on his companions, he resisted his instinct for conversation. In due course the orchestra stopped for refreshments, and Lacey went outside to one of the smoking booths to engage with his pipe. Eva opinioned to Garrick that Ranelagh was a big improvement on the Vauxhall Gardens further down river, which was often plagued with yobbery and oafishness. After both Garrick and Johnson nodded their agreement, they all rose from the booth to join Lacey outside for a stroll through the lighted gardens. There were several occasions when Garrick was recognised and approached. Obviously enjoying the recognition, Garrick dealt with these intrusions with great charm and politeness. At one point Johnson's jealousy fleetingly surfaced, critically suggesting to Garrick he should sometimes be less strident when delivering his lines on stage.

Garrick grinned good naturedly at Johnson, replying that Johnson would be forever his tutor and himself the pupil. Johnson sharply reminded Garrick that if all he ever heard was praise without criticism, then eventually that praise would become worthless.

By late afternoon James Lacey instructed his carriage men to transport his guests back to Covent Garden, as he had some remaining business to attend to at Ranelagh. Going back east along Piccadilly, the passengers once again had the opportunity to admire the beautiful Palladian architecture of Burlington House to their left. They went on to pass through Leicester Fields, before entering a maze of lanes taking them past the open yards of the numerous carriage makers in Long Acre. They finished their journey by passing swiftly through Covent Garden, and entering the fine residential district of Southampton Street.

After assisting Eva in alighting from the carriage, Garrick with his usual charm, persuaded the liveried footmen to extend their journey further east to Temple Bar. This was in order to drop off his good friend nearer to Gough Square. Dismounting from the carriage at Temple Bar a few minutes later, Johnson had a distinct spring in his step despite his lack of sleep. A combination of his completion of the Dictionary, the pleasant afternoon in Ranelegh, and an evening to look forward to at his precious Ivy Lane Club, brought a triple boost to his morale.

The Ivy Lane Club had been founded by Johnson six years earlier. It was a period when the stressful pressure of working on the Dictionary, plus the demoralising effects of his wife's decline, had compounded his feelings of lonely isolation. Occasional chance meetings in coffee houses were not enough for him. He needed to meet his friends regularly for lively debates. It was vital for his mental health that he could lose himself, for just a few hours, in order to forget painful reflections. So he persuaded a few select friends to meet once a week at the King's Head, a beefsteak house in Ivy Lane, dominated by the shadow of Wren's magnificent St Paul's Cathedral. The large imposing figure of Johnson, strode purposefully down the length of Fleet Street towards the King's Head. Straight ahead of him, the splendid majestic dome of St Paul's was silhouetted in the darkening early evening sky. On entering the tavern Johnson was taken by surprise, for in addition to the usual members of the Club, there were several other acquaintances, all obviously gathered together in his honour. Among the regular Club members seated in their usual corner alcove, were legal expert Sir John Hawkins, John Hawkesworth, a talented professional writer whom Johnson had actively encouraged, and Doctor Richard Bathurst.

Bathurst was a gentle soul who seemed to underachieve financially, and had lodged intermittently at Gough Square when his funds were low. Also present were two of the Dictionary backers. Robert Dodsley, Johnson's good friend and bookseller, who had originally approached him with the Dictionary project, and fellow bookseller Thomas Longman. Completing the company of non-club members, were Dictionary assistants and lodgers at Gough Square, Victor Peyton and Alexander Macbean, Johnson's printer friend William Strahan and young writer Charlotte Lennox. Among a furore of cheering and backslapping, a surprised and secretly delighted Johnson was shown to his regular seat. A feast of beef, bacon and eggs, followed by apple pie washed down with rum, whisky and wine, was served at the table. Throughout the meal speeches were made by Robert Dodsley and Charlotte Lennox. Their kind words praised Johnson's tenacity in finishing the Dictionary, his intelligence and robust common sense, and lastly his willingness to help others who were struggling for Literary recognition. Charlotte Lennox was one such beneficiary of Johnson's patronage. Like Johnson she was definitely an eccentric outsider, and bright young spirits like her were good medicine for Johnson. He admired her energy and independence of spirit, plus her realistic portrayals of women's expectations in her novels. After the meal, Johnson occupied his favourite tavern throne, and then the discussions and intellectual debate began. Subjects as diverse as oratory, flattery, Shakespeare, cider, Jesus Christ, money, politics, theatre, literature and witchcraft, came up for analysis. Johnson was now in full stride, his exactness of expression enabling him to reason, discuss, dictate and control the debates, all the while deploying his rich fund of humour to soften the disagreements.

When asked by Charlotte Lennox what made a good author, Johnson replied that what was important was not the technique of the writing but the spirit of the writer. Thomas Longman ventured to say that Garrick's latest play was worth seeing. Johnston countered saying 'Worth seeing yes, but not worth going to see'. When asked his opinion on the present unpopularity of the Government, Johnson discoursed that in any judgement of the ruling class, you should always balance the corrupt self perpetuating tendencies of any Government that stifled individual freedom, against the uninformed public resentment and simplistic idealism of the masses.

The evenings entertainment was momentarily threatened when closing time approached. This threat was countered when Charlotte Lennox suggested that the Devil Tavern near Temple Bar, often stayed open beyond the midnight hour. Only the Dictionary syndicate members Robert Dodsley and Thomas Longman declined, as the rest of the company trundled down Ludgate Hill in two Hackney Coaches, making their way towards Fleet Street and Temple Bar. Once inside the Tavern, the night and early hours passed in pleasant conversation and harmless mirth. At five in the morning Johnson was still playing to his much diminished gallery, his face shining with contented goodwill. Never one to go to bed early, he often chastised himself for rising from his slumbers at midday, feeling that he was wasting valuable time in which he could be doing something more worthy. Ideally he would have liked to have gone without sleep altogether, for the longer he could stay up, the longer he could delay confronting the desolate silence he so dreaded in the early hours at Gough Square. Now in the tavern only Johnson, Sir John Hawkins, and Charlotte Lennox were still awake. Hawkesworth, Peyton Macbean, Bathurst and Strahan, were all in various states of slumber along with some of the waiters.

Raising enough energy to order one more round of coffee, Lennox gently nudged the sleepers awake as John Hawkins settled the bill for the evening. By the time the door creaked open to signal their departure, the day was beginning to dawn with bright sunshine. Blinking into the light, the revellers mumbled their goodbyes and set off towards their respective dwellings. Johnson, Macbean, Peyton, and Bathurst turned eastwards, making their way slowly along Fleet Street towards Gough Square. As they walked, Johnson drew in a deep breath of the early morning air; for on the dawning of this bright spring day in his beloved London, Samuel Johnson was for once at peace with himself and enjoying existence.

5

LONDON
FEBRUARY 1844

T he early morning air blew cold, smelly and damp across the dark and misty London streets. The occasional shadow and sound of footsteps were the only reminders that the city housed a population of two million people. The circumstances in which that mass of humanity existed varied enormously, for London, in becoming the richest city in the world, carried many victims in its wake. Walking briskly along the New Road, a small, slight, boyish-looking individual, made his way through the dim light cast by the intermittent gas lamps. The man was dressed in a flamboyant blue cloak with velvet lapels, part of which was thrown over his shoulder for fashionable effect. On the outside looking in, the much celebrated young author Charles Dickens had much to be pleased about, as a string of literary classics produced by the age of 32 had catapulted his literary career towards fame and fortune. As he walked towards his house at Number One Devonshire Terrace – opposite Regents Park – he was returning from one of his habitual nocturnal walks. He made these marathon excursions in search of inspiration, using his observations to fire his considerable imagination in preparation for his next best seller. Number One Devonshire Terrace was a grand house with the front door and exterior railings painted in Dickens favourite colour of bright green, with its square garden being protected by a high wall. It had two floors containing thirteen rooms that were well furnished with candelabra, rosewood chairs covered with satin, silk curtains and large mirrors. Dickens shared this house with his wife Catherine, his five children, his sister-in-law Georgina, and four domestic servants.

After entering the house at just gone 4 o'clock in the morning, he walked swiftly in the direction of his study. Though he had expended much energy on his walk, he was still feeling restless and slightly troubled, the nagging anxiety with which he was familiar had still not abated. His father John Dickens was still making further financial demands on him, plus the responsibility of his fast growing family was also weighing heavily. Also the proceeds of his books, though lucrative, could never seem to soothe his financial insecurities. These insecurities were deeply rooted in his childhood experience, the traumatic result of being the son of a father who had habitually lived above his means. This led at one time to his father being imprisoned in the infamous

Marshalsea Debtors Prison. Dickens never forgot the shame this brought upon the family, and the devastating impact on his lower middle class upbringing. Having to move into less expensive housing at that time, plus the negative impact it had inflicted on his education at a crucial period, had left permanent mental scars.

These financial panic attacks induced in him the constant need to be on the move, not only in terms of exercise and travel, but also in his work. The publishing of each successful book provided temporary comfort in helping to ease his irrational fears of financial ruin and poverty. The themes of neglect and deprivation were becoming a constant topic in his stories, as he began to witness the full horrors of the destitute poor on his many excursions into the dark corners of London existence.

His friendship with fellow literary giant Thomas Carlyle, a radical humanitarian, helped to sharpen and focus his own social conscience and appetite for radical reform. Dickens felt increasingly that in his writing he could highlight the plight of the poor, with the intention of bringing pressure to bear on those holding the levers of power, in order to prick the consciences of the privileged. As he sat at his desk Dickens's attention was drawn to a sealed envelope that had been placed on his desk in his absence.

After carefully breaking the seal, Dickens removed two folded sheets of paper and proceeded to read them. Dickens slowly absorbed the details of the correspondence, reading the letter through twice, and deliberating on its implications. The letter was from Benjamin Disraeli, a 40-year-old Conservative politician, who had recently created a stir in political circles by forming a split in his party with the radical Young

Conservative Movement. On the few occasions when their paths had crossed, Dickens had found him a curious mix of affectation and arrogance, capable of either brilliant or vacuous conversation depending on his mood. Disraeli was requesting a meeting with Dickens that afternoon, in order to further his research as regards social deprivation in the poorer classes. From his experience as a young parliamentary reporter, Dickens held politicians in general as beneath contempt, but he realised that he had to put these feelings aside if he was going to achieve his aims of social reform for the poor. Dickens swiftly penned his reply, stating that he would be at home at 3 o'clock that afternoon. Dickens then rose from his desk and retired to his bedroom in order to get some sleep.

At 8 o'clock that morning just a mile south of Dickens House, Benjamin Disraeli sat his breakfast table in Grosvenor Gate, Park Lane. Sitting opposite was his wife Mary Anne, 12 years his senior, they had married five years earlier, soon after her first husband had died. Born into a prosperous Jewish family, Disraeli had lived the life of the rich London socialite, foreign travel, country houses, summer parties and fine dining had been his staple diet. But though enjoying these privileges, he had always felt he was destined for a more noble higher calling. At first encouraged by his book loving father, he had felt literary fame was to be his destiny, but his early published works had received mixed reviews and were not to everyone's taste.

Living his life as if money was no object, his outgoings had been far exceeding his income, resulting in some massive debts and fractured friendships. He had realised that if he was going to achieve something that was lasting and worthy, he would have to make the most of his gifts of eloquence and oratory. Not being short of political connections, the opportunities to enter the world of parliament began to open despite the anti-Semitic prejudices that existed in some quarters. Now sitting at his window overlooking Hyde Park, Disraeli felt content with his progress in the Commons. He was also content with his social life and marriage, plus the house at Grosvenor Gate that his wife, formerly a rich widow, had brought to their union. To an outsider it was rather a pretentious house, the large downstairs dining room was painted a dull brown, and hung with conventional paintings. While upstairs the huge L shaped drawing room was a blaze of splendor, vulgar crimson Wilton carpets, gold silk damask curtains and heavy gilt-framed mirrors. As well as a coachman, there were as many as eight indoor servants all dressed in bright brown livery. The precious necessity of plentiful clean water was laid on to the kitchen area and to the upper floors, supplied by pipes drawing from large covered storage tanks. There was much laughter and teasing between Disraeli and his wife in the duration of the breakfast, as they indulged in high society gossip, and planned their party weekends. At the end of the breakfast they both rose from the table in order to take their regular constitutional walk in Hyde Park.

Charles Dickens had not resided long in his bedroom, his customary restlessness, combined with thoughts on his arranged meeting with Disraeli, had made sleep impossible. He was also troubled by the malaise affecting his wife after the birth of his latest child the previous month.

Her health after all her pregnancies thus far, had seen the same pattern of depression and inertia, and Dickens somewhat unsympathetic, had found her condition frustrating and dispiriting.

Unable to sleep, Dickens had quickly washed and dressed, using the same privileged water supply arrangements as were available at the house of Disraeli. After a quick breakfast of toast and coffee, he had scribbled on another note of paper and addressed the envelope to his friend Thomas Carlyle. He then handed two letters to his servant, one for Carlyle in Cheyne Row, Chelsea, the other to Disraeli in Park Lane, instructing that they should be delivered immediately by hand. He had then retired to the parlour where his children were playing games with one of the maids and learning to dance. Dickens joined in immediately, eager to enter their world of childhood and innocence, losing himself in their appreciation of novel experience. He spent the next hour in blissful absorption with his children, before leaving the parlour just as the big clock in the hall struck 11 o' clock. After briefly going to his bedroom to check on his wife, Catherine, who was sleeping soundly, he briskly donned his hat and left the house.

Meanwhile in Hyde Park, Benjamin Disraeli strolled happily with his wife Mary Anne. As was their custom when time and climate allowed, they would walk the full circuit of the park, though absorbed in their conversation they would still be appreciative of what the park had to offer. A vast area of grass and trees in the very heart of the city, Hyde Park was a country gentleman's park transported to the centre of the capital. As Disraeli and his wife walked past the waters of the Serpentine, they were hailed by wealthy people in their carriages. Elegant women wearing silks and laces, nodded their recognition as powdered attendants held on to their trailing dresses.

The wide avenue of Rotten Row, which threaded through the park, was highly populated with magnificent horses ridden by fashionably dressed ladies and their matrons. Though the skies were dull, the day was still and dry, with the effects of the cool temperatures easily offset by adequate clothing. As they paused briefly by the Serpentine, Disraeli gently teased his wife by stating that he had married her for money, before hastening to reassure her that if he married her again it would be for love. Mary Anne laughingly said that she would have no hesitation in pushing Disraeli into the lake if his cheek persisted, and after pretending to do so, she took Disraeli's arm and walked on. On their return to Grosvenor Gate, Disraeli was handed a letter from the footman, after a brief examination of the envelope, Disraeli excused himself and retired to his study.

Upon leaving Devonshire Terrace, Charles Dickens turned right along the New Road, then right again into the rural pastures of Tottenham Court Road, heading towards the densely populated district of Westminster. He was hoping that he would be meeting his friend Thomas Carlyle in the area of Westminster Bridge at 12 o'clock, a suggestion he had made in the written note he had dispatched that very morning. Before meeting Disraeli that afternoon, Dickens had felt that he needed some advice from his radical friend, plus a bit more personal knowledge of Disraeli. Thomas Carlyle had crossed political swords with Disraeli on several occasions, and was sure to have some valuable insight.

As Dickens walked, his keen observant eye missed nothing. All human life paraded in the London streets, and the characters and situations he encountered as he walked, slipped into his imagination. From the old women selling apples and matches, the costermongers with their carts selling flowers, fish and muffins, to the occasional glimpses of the barefoot feral children that slept in the alleys and beneath the bridges – nothing escaped his curious gaze. Dickens proceeded to head south, bypassing the crowded slum district of St Giles and entering the recently developed Trafalgar Square. This wide area was dominated by the tall Corinthian Column and statue of Lord Nelson, and overlooked by the National Gallery. Having seen it many times on his countless excursions, Dickens pressed on through the incessant streams of horse-drawn traffic and bustling pavements. Entering Whitehall, he passed several Government offices as he neared the Houses of Parliament and Westminster Bridge. As he approached the River Thames, a pale yellow fog was rolling up from it's riverbanks. The obnoxious stink in the air had grown more thick and strong with each step nearer to the river, getting to the point where Dickens now found it almost unbearable. This was no surprise, as all the sewers and pollution of the largest city in the world flowed within the Thames. This bred epidemic disease among the urban population, as a combination of human waste, ammonia, cyanide and carbolic acid formed a highly toxic cocktail. The water itself was turgid and dark, its distinctive smell was that of hydrogen, created by the removal of oxygen from the water.

As Dickens waited near Westminster Bridge, he glanced up at the ongoing construction of the new Palace of Westminster. Designed by architects Charles Barry and Augustus Pugin, it was already showing all the signs of being a Gothic masterpiece. Dickens also noticed that the windows of the various Government buildings were hung with heavy drapes soaked in chlorine, this was in a vain attempt to dilute the impact of the offensive odours. The dark sludgy waters of the River Thames exerted a morbid fascination on Dickens, and as he turned again to gaze at it's black stinking inkiness, he realised that it had featured prominently in most of his successful novels thus far. As he waited for his friend, he was again struck by the bustling energy of the capital city. Above the sound of ships hooting in the distance, there was the clatter of hooves on the cobbles, the creak of hackney carriages, and the cries of street hawkers. The area was thronged with busy people: men in tall hats and greatcoats, errand boys, ladies in bonnets and shawls. At 12 o'clock precisely, a distinguished bearded man with a shock of grey hair, alighted from a horse drawn cab directly opposite Westminster Bridge. Dickens recognised his friend immediately and advanced towards him.

After thanking him for coming at such short notice, and asking after the welfare of Carlyle's wife Jane, Dickens suggested they should take the hospitality of the Red Lion public house in Parliament Street. It was an establishment known for the quality of its real ale, and Dickens knew it well. After handing over two pennies for two pints of ale, Dickens led Carlyle to some seating in front of an open fire, where the two men proceeded to engage in deep conversation. Dickens, animated and talking quickly, asked for more information on Disraeli, while Carlyle's response was measured and thoughtful. When Carlyle had received Dickens's letter mentioning Disraeli, he had been immediately interested. He told Dickens that Disraeli was clever, and that unlike the self deluded Gladstone, Disraeli was a charlatan and he knew it. Carlyle called him the Hebrew Conjurer, driven by ambition and capable of supreme oratory. Carlyle concluded his analysis by expressing doubts whether the views that Disraeli expressed so elegantly, are altogether sincerely held. Carlyle then went on to say that Dickens should still use

Disraeli in his crusade for social reform, as his eloquence would give useful publicity to the cause. After leaving the tavern and saying their goodbyes, Dickens headed northwards lost in his thoughts, being uncharacteristically oblivious to the crowds as he made his way home.

Back in his study at Grosvenor Gate, Disraeli leaned backwards in his chair, he was leafing a book bound in red cloth, with a gilt design on the cover and full colour etchings inside, it was indeed a handsome volume. The book was titled *A Christmas Carol* and it was the latest successful publication from Charles Dickens. Disraeli had read the book over the recent Christmas, and its theme of redemption after revealing the two wretched poor children 'Ignorance and Want' had been of great interest to him.

The plight of the poor had occupied his thoughts greatly in recent months, sowing the seed of an idea for his own new book called *Sybil or the Two Nations* highlighting the contrast between the rich and the poor. The seemingly perverse idea that the numbers of poor were increasing as the country became more wealthy, was gaining credence among radical reformers and had particularly struck a cord with Disraeli. Now at the mature age of 40, and with his parliamentary career beginning to blossom, Disraeli was beginning to see his calling being crystallised into something tangible and lasting. Disraeli had been heartened to receive Dickens's positive reply to his request for an audience with the author, for he knew that Dickens was a commited authority on the state of the poor and could educate him greatly. Disraeli was no fool, he realised that serious men like Dickens did not much care for rich arrogant dandies like himself. But he also knew that he was in a position to prove that the erratic frivolous fancies of his youth were now past, and that the underlying seriousness and intelligence that he had always possessed, could now come to palpable fruition.

Disraeli put down his copy of *A Christmas Carol* and proceeded to study two sheets of foolscap paper, the content of those sheets made distressing reading. They stated that the average age of mortality for the London poor was 22, and that almost half the funerals in the capital were of children under the age of 10. In the poorest districts 70,000 houses had no access to mains water, having to rely on polluted wells, leading to regular outbreaks of typhoid fever, dysentery, cholera, and smallpox.

As Disraeli read the dreadful details, he increasingly realised that London incorporated two tribes: rich and poor, living side by side without noticing each other's existence. At 2 o'clock Disraeli rose from his desk and summoned his coachman, for he did not want to be late for his appointment.

Charles Dickens had returned from his lunchtime rendezvous with Thomas Carlyle in a positive mood. Though not prepared to accept Disraeli as a friend, he had decided to make use of Disraeli's presentation skills and position, in order to increase the awareness of the problem poor. After a light lunch of bread and fish, he retired to his quarters in order to wash and change. Dickens emerged from his rooms wearing a dark suit, red bow tie and white shirt, he then entered the parlour where his wife Catherine, accompanied by her maid Anne Brown, were residing in comfy chairs. Though still poorly, Catherine seemed a touch brighter in herself, seeming to be interested in her husband's approaching liason with Disraeli.

Small and plump, her pretty features looked tired and drawn as she listened attentively to her husband's account of Disraeli's written request. Dickens briefly outlined his motives and intentions, and then told her of the meeting with their friend Carlyle, and the thoughtful observations that the radical thinker opinioned. At 3 o'clock Dickens rose from his chair, and excused himself from the parlour in order to receive his visitor.

Benjamin Disraeli looked at himself in the mirror, dressed in a dark bottle green frock coat, worn over a waistcoat covered with glittering chains, he cut a slightly exotic figure. Of slender build and slightly stooped, his pale complexion, intensely dark eyes and long black hair set in curls, provided a riveting contrast. Leaving his house in Park Lane, his coachman was soon heading up the busy artery that was Gloucester Place, heading towards Regents Park and North London. The traffic congestion was appalling, the daily congested mix of crowded horse drawn Omnibuses, one horse cabs, sedate private carriages and animal herds, creating their usual frustrating log jam.

The squared granite paving on the roads was buried daily under a vast quantity of hay, straw, horse dung and urine. Sitting in the carriage Disraeli glanced at his fob watch, realising he was going to be a little late, he mentally prepared himself for the meeting. By the time his carriage finally turned right into New Road, Disraeli was resolute in his determination that the meeting would produce a positive outcome. Disraeli was all of 20 minutes late by the time he entered Charles Dickens's house, and immediately apologised graciously to Dickens for his late arrival. Dickens shook his hand politely, and then led Disraeli to the parlour to briefly introduce him to Catherine, before moving briskly on to the drawing room. After some initial small talk about traffic congestion, the two men were served a glass of red wine as they took their seats in front of the fire. Though they had met from time to time on various literary occasions, the two men had rarely spoken to each other, so there was an initial period of guarded reserve. After Disraeli had complimented Dickens on his latest successful publication of *A Christmas Carol* he went on to say that after reading it over the Christmas holiday, he had felt compelled to request a meeting with Dickens, and was grateful it had been granted.

At this point Dickens came straight to the point, 'Which brings us to the reasons as to why you requested it'. Disraeli paused for a moment before replying 'You write about the London poor with great imagination, but I happen to know that you do not just novelise the condition of Victorian England, that indeed you actively engage with the social issues of the day'. Dickens replied immediately 'It is a deplorable circumstance in this country that depresses me daily, believe me when I tell you there is no need for imagination when you see the reality'. Disraeli could see immediately in Dickens facial expression, the depth of his disgust.

Disraeli responded 'It is the ever growing population of the poor that I find most disappointing, why is poverty increasing in London, after all it is the greatest capital city on earth and the centre of international trade and finance' Dickens answered stridently 'London, Mr Disraeli, is a city based on money and power, and those unfortunates who have neither, are literally degraded and stripped of all human decency by a city that has no other purpose except greed.' Disraeli absorbed these comments reflectively, only the sound of the log fire crackling in the grate breaking the temporary silence. Disraeli expanded on his motivation, 'Mr Dickens, I am increasingly seeing this as my mission in politics, to effect radical policies in order to make a difference to those unfortunate people.' Dickens sighed wearily, he knew from his previous experience as a Parliamentary writer that fine words were the most valued commodity in those exalted corridors of power, with meaningful action often coming a poor second. Disraeli sensed Dickens skepticism immediately, realising that the great writer was obviously cynical of statesmen whom democracy had degraded into politcians. The silence was finally broken by Dickens, 'Everywhere I turn I see a system that fails, surely any decent, civilized country can at least provide for its poorest unfortunates basic sanitation, education and decent housing.'

The room went silent once more as Dickens stopped talking and stared sullenly into the fire. Disraeli remained quietly thoughtful as he digested the remarks made by Dickens, while at the same time being mildly diverted by the effect of the flickering firelight dancing on the features of Dickens's half-turned face. Before Disraeli could offer his response, Dickens's eyes suddenly adopted a look of intensity before stating stridently 'Why is it that when you speak to any traveller from the continent, he will tell you that the London poor seem somehow more crushed and degraded than the needy from their own country, seeming to be more sick and hungry, with lives barren of all meaning and faith.' This time Disraeli did not delay in replying 'I fervently believe that the health and education of the people is the foundation upon which all their happiness depends, and I would see it as my duty to secure the social welfare of the whole nation.'

Dickens responded 'With respect Mr Disraeli you are a product of the system and the system as it stands frequently disgusts me'. Disraeli waited momentarily before enquiring 'Would you seriously advocate revolution?'. Dickens paused reflectively as the servant refilled their wine glasses, before answering 'If that is what it would take to change the circumstances of the poor, then yes.' Disraeli took a sip of his wine and lapsed into deep thought as he studied the intense young author before him. It was obvious that Dickens's beliefs were passionately held but not necessarily carefully considered. Disraeli finally gave his thoughtfully worded answer, 'I genuinely believe that the poor and lowly paid of this country would always choose social improvement over political equality.' Dickens stared fixedly back into the fire before replying 'The reality of the situation makes me seriously doubt you can have one without the other.'

Seeking to convince Dickens that there was another way Disraeli went on 'As you have always used your formidable imagination in writing your novels, I as a young Conservative will endeavour to do likewise in my politics.' Dickens looked questioningly at his guest, patiently waiting for Disraeli to continue. Disraeli needed little encouragement to expand 'I believe we should preserve all that is good in our constitution, and be ruthlessly radical in removing all that is bad.' Before Dickens could respond Disraeli gently went on 'Please do not take me lightly, if you doubt my sincerity take me now to see the things that you have seen, in order that I can feel the way you feel.'

Dickens was initially taken aback by Disraeli's demand and at first suggested that it would be too dangerous with nightfall fast approaching. But Disraeli was determinedly persuasive, assuring

Dickens of full protection from danger by mentioning his burly coachman. Suddenly remembering the advice of his friend Carlyle and the possible benefits of Disraeli's eloquence and profile, Dickens finally agreed to Disraeli's surprise request. Twenty minutes later the carriage belonging to Disraeli was heading down the New Road.

In addition to Disraeli's coach driver there were three other men travelling; Disraeli, Dickens, and one of his young servants. The winter daylight was fading fast as Disraeli gazed out of the carriage window, being lost in his own thoughts, there was a pensive silence within the carriage. He had realised early on in his conversation with Dickens, that merely talking about the London poor would not be enough. If he was going to achieve his objectives and convince radical cynics like Dickens, he could not remain emotionally detached from the harsh realities of deprivation. As the carriage rattled down Tottenham Court Road, Disraeli had at first supposed they were heading for the slum back streets of Westminster. These slums were often mentioned within the confines of Parliament from time to time, but always physically avoided by the politicians as they travelled back and forth. But after entering the busy thoroughfare of Charing Cross, Dickens instructed the coachman to turn left by the church of St Giles.

Dickens had decided that this was an opportunity too good to be missed, and was directing the carriage to the Rookeries of St Giles. This desolate area was an island of cellars and abandoned tenements, ringed by a congregation of yards, courts and alleys. Disraeli suddenly felt the atmosphere change as the traffic noise of Charing Cross was abruptly cut off, and an oppressive menacing darkness began to envelop.

Disraeli turned to Dickens and enquired 'Where is this?' Dickens gave him the benefit of his knowledge 'The St Giles Rookeries, an area of old gutted houses that have been left as empty shells for the poor to inherit.' Disraeli peered into the gloom 'But I cannot see anyone.' Dickens assured him, 'Believe me Mr Disraeli, they are everywhere.'

As the carriage rolled slowly on, Disraeli became aware of an overpowering stench of stale bodies and raw sewage, and with his eyes growing accustomed to the darkness, he began to pick out pale shapes among the shadows. All four men on the carriage covered their mouths and noses, Dickens and Disraeli used their cloaks, while up top the coachman and servant wore their cravats as a mask. Peering into the gloom, Disraeli could just make out the ghostly shapes of decaying tenements with their smashed windows stuffed with rags and paper. Then came the shouting; men, women and children, all begging as one. Disraeli could see through the windows as many as 50 people to a room, some too weak and feeble to notice their presence. In front of the houses the streets was littered with tin pots, kettles, old clothes, cast-off shoes, dead cats and dogs.

Troops of pale wide eyed children could be seen crouched on filthy staircases, families huddling close, their heads hanging, their bodies shaking with cold. Though Dickens had seen such squalor and human misery many times, it never failed to fill him with a frustrating mix of pity, revulsion and anger. As for Disraeli he had seen enough, his face was pale and shocked, his cold hands shaking and clammy.

Aware of Disraeli's distress Dickens instructed the coachman to swiftly move on, with the coach soon entering the wide expanse of Trafalgar Square. Feeling quite ill, Disraeli asked the coachman to stop so that he could recover his equilibrium. Dickens pulled a flask of water from his coat and offered it to a grateful Disraeli. As Disraeli quietly sipped, Dickens offered an observation 'It is a tragedy of our times is it not, that a city so wealthy and large can conceal in its depths so much famine filth and disease.' Disraeli staring down at the floor of the carriage muttered faintly 'We do indeed inhabit two nations, totally ignorant of each others thoughts and feelings.' Dickens went on 'Just five minutes away from the richest thoroughfares in London, we have citizens who live in profound ignorance and perfect barbarism.' Disraeli looked up at Dickens, his voice shaking 'When I looked at those children's vacant expressions I felt I was seeing drowning people; how do you save them? Who to save first?' Dickens replied solemnly 'We see the shape of the city from the shadow that it casts, it is the spiritual element that is drowning in those children.'

Disraeli felt he knew the answer. 'In addition to social reform they need to feel a part of this nation, to be given a faith in the church, and a pride in crown and country – that will be my path.' The mood was sombre on the journey back to Dickens house, with both men deeply thoughtful and not inclined to conversation. Nearing Dickens's house, Disraeli broke his silence. 'Mr Dickens, please do not underestimate me. You may not like to hear this but there are issues in this world we see the same, indeed in many ways I could be you with a white silk handkerchief.' Dickens smiled at this analogy but made no comment. As Dickens alighted from the carriage, Disraeli spoke to him through the open window. 'You can depend on it that my political career will be targeted on this abomination, and I swear to you now that I will make an impact.'

Dickens looked earnestly back at Disraeli's pale face 'Every fibre of my being wants to believe you will be successful, but I fear it will be the triumph of hope over experience.'

Disraeli smiled reassuringly and declared 'Justice is truth in action.' Dickens watched the coach slowly disappear into the cold evening mist.

6

LONDON
SEPTEMBER 1940

The sun rose brightly over London, swiftly burning away the early morning September haze. A steady two-way stream of cars and buses flowed across London Bridge. Normally the bridge would be swarmed with midweek commuters, making their way to the city offices where they made their living, but this was a Saturday. The population of Great Britain had increased by more than five million between the First and Second World Wars. Of these one-third lived in London or worked there, creating a population of 8.2 million, one and a half million more than New York. Over this period 1.2

million houses had been built to accommodate the ever increasing inhabitants. A quarter of the country's imports passed through the Port of London, while the manufacturing output of London's factories was the largest in the country. The wealth of the world flowed through the narrow, crooked streets of the square mile, the original ancient core from which London spread it's outward tentacles. Only a few people actually lived among the banks, exchanges and insurance companies, but every weekday morning, hundreds of thousands flowed in to ensure the financial wheels kept in motion.

On the first casual glance, everything appeared normal on this fine sunny morning, the trains and buses were running, people were joking with their regular newspaper vendors, and the food markets of Billingsgate, Smithfield and Covent Garden appeared to be functioning. But if you looked closely at the expressions and mannerisms of the people, it was possible to detect an underlying anxiety and forced cheerfulness. A bird's-eye view of the landscape revealed more. Large, irregularly shaped meandering trenches scarred the landscape, and enormous silver Barrage balloons attached to metal cables, drifted on the morning breeze. Back on the ground, thousands of sandbags hugged the contours of the buildings. These were the clues that confirmed that London, the biggest, greatest city in the world, was continuing to exist and function, while under the most extreme peril.

A couple of miles south west of London Bridge stood No 10 Downing Street, home to British Prime Ministers for the previous 200 years. In the upstairs bedroom, Winston Churchill was already well into his 15 hour working day, dictating to his secretary, while wearing a resplendent patterned dressing gown. Making urgent phone calls, and scribbling strategies on bits of paper, at 66 years of age he was displaying the energy of someone half his years. Appointed Prime Minister, leading a war time Coalition Government, he felt with awe-inspiring certainty, that all his past life had been but a preparation for this hour and this trial.

Born in the magnificent Baroque structure that was Blenheim Palace in Oxfordshire – built in gratitude for his heroic victorious ancestor, The Duke of Marlborough – Winston Churchill had no doubts about the British Empire and his place in the clutches of history. Finally satisfied that his initial early morning business was finalised, he dismissed his secretary and retired to the bathroom. As he wallowed in his customary morning bath, it occurred to him that in these dangerous uncertain times, he felt more exhilarated than at any time in his last 20 years. Now in total command of all military operations, he felt he could put to bed his personal demons relating to the Dardanelles in World War One. At that time he had tried to enforce a strategy from a subordinate position, but not receiving full commitment from his superiors, the plan had been modified, resulting in disastrous and catastrophic loss of life. The whole episode had been calamitous for both his reputation, and not least his political career. Removed from political office, he had plunged into one of his 'black dog' depressions, and sought consolation in painting watercolours. At that time in his early 40s, he eventually realised the only route to redemption was in active service. Drawing on his earlier experiences in the Boer War, he had seen out World War One commanding a battalion of Royal Scots Fusiliers.

In the intervening 'wilderness years' he had retreated to Chartwell, his expensive country house in Kent, writing books on British History, building walls in the extensive grounds, and brooding about past and future. He had been kept up to speed in world events, by the numerous politicians who he had invited as guests on a regular basis.

As he stood in front of the mirror adjusting his bow tie, he realised it had been his position as an objective spectator, that had given him the advantage of sensing the Nazi menace before everyone else. He had realised early on that the Nazi regime would not be stopped by ingratiating appeasement, but by adopting a position of strength through rearmament, particularly aircraft production. He had proved to be the Prophet of Truth, as with each German invasion, his steady unremitting forecasts came to pass. The failed appeasement policy of Conservative Prime Minister Neville Chamberlain was finally there for all to see, as the German Fuhrer Adolf Hitler, pushed his armies through mainland Europe. With Chamberlain losing the confidence of the House of Commons, Churchill now found himself heading up his hand picked Coalition Government, determined to maintain Britain's island identity or die in the attempt.

His appointment as Prime Minister had proved popular with the general public, his broadcast speeches in particular steeling the nation, filling it with patriotic pride, quiet determination, and adrenaline charged courage. Making his way to the spacious kitchen quarters in Downing Street, he lit his first Havana cigar of the day. As he gazed out of a large plate glassed window overlooking the Treasury buildings, he made some rapid mental calculations on the present state of affairs.

France had fallen, German armies across the channel were poised to strike, Italy had declared war on Britain also.

Months earlier, the massive evacuation of Dunkirk had seemed like Britain had snatched a small victory from the jaws of a massive defeat, but it would take months before the factories could replace the munitions lost in that operation.

On the plus side there was the Channel, that little stretch of water that had historically served Britain so well. There was also the stoical nature of the majority of British citizens, who seemed more willing to have their great island reduced to dust, than surrender to the Nazi Regime. He also took great comfort from his close relationship with Franklin D. Roosevelt the American President – already their supply boats were providing valuable weapons and equipment. Not least there was the superlative skill and daring of the RAF pilots, who had already proved more than a match for the Luftwaffe, in the initial confrontations over the south coast. Finally there was the fine workings of the War Cabinet and Coalition Government. The combination of all the talents had so far worked together supremely. He was interrupted from these thoughts by the War Cabinet secretary Edward Bridges, reminding him that there was a meeting scheduled above the Cabinet War Rooms at 11am. Stubbing out his cigar, he followed the secretary through to the corridors of power.

The small east end artery that was Three Colts Lane, lay approximately two and a half miles north east of the grand government buildings of Downing Street. Tucked away behind Bethnal Green Road, alongside the railway arches, it was a world away from the political power struggles of Whitehall.

The lane ran parallel to the railway line that carried the weekly office workers into Liverpool Street Station, the trains providing a constant noisy backdrop to the daily existence of the neighbourhood. Though none of the houses had hot water or inside toilets, the dwellings at the eastern end of the lane were particularly dark and dingy, their gardens no more than a backyard. Circumstances had improved massively for the London poor from Victorian times, but if you were unemployed or among the lowest paid, then life was still particularly grim. Very few starved or walked the streets naked, but food was minimal for these people, and their clothes were discoloured and threadbare. Three Colts Lane was definitely a place you could call a community. Everyone knew their neighbours by name and looked out for one another, with close knit families living just a few doors away from each other.

For the people that lived there, the lane itself was a communal public place, where children were always out playing marbles and hopscotch, and the adults passed the time of day with one another. It was not unusual for people to bring out their chairs on warm summer evenings, and chat for hours on the pavements. At the western end of the thoroughfare, the houses, though hardly luxurious, were generally larger with bigger gardens. It was in the garden of one of these houses, that a small stocky man of middle age dug vigorously into the soil. In an area that had more than its fair share of characters, Ted Harrison was an exceptional individual. Intelligently streetwise, resourceful and energetic, he was a serious man for serious times. Unlike his lifelong friend, jovial Harry Carter, he had decided early on, that life was a serious business and that frivolity had little place in it. He had not always felt like that, but his experiences in World War One at Flanders, plus the loss of two brothers in the conflict, had steeled and chastened him. Ever since those horrific times, he had accepted the cards that life dealt him, never wasting time wishing that he had been born rich, dealing pragmatically with existence as it was, not what he would wish it to be.

At the bottom of the garden stood a large pen full of ducks and chickens, and to the right of it stood two curved sections of corrugated iron that had been bolted together at the top.

This contraption was called an Anderson shelter, designed to offer protection from Hitler's bombs, and offered for free by the Government, if you were fortunate enough to have a garden. The main problem was when erected they had no drainage, and tended to flood at the first sign of heavy rain, consequently they needed to be constantly baled out and maintained. Ted was constantly trying to find ways to make his shelter more rainproof, and it was in this painstaking endeavour that he was now actively engaged. Watching him, with his elbows planted firmly on the fence, was old Jack Walker, his longtime neighbour. Ted was now digging a new three foot deep ditch, in order to sink his shelter into the ground. Building up a sweat, Ted listened patiently to Jack's well meant advice, knowing full well that he would be asked to drain Jack's shelter afterwards. The welcoming sight of Ted's teenage daughter Rita, entering the garden carrying two mugs of tea, helped to raise his spirits. Handing over the two mugs of hot liquid to both Ted and Jack, Rita informed them that her mum was still in the queue at the butchers, which trailed half the length of Roman Road.

That week there had been some increased sporadic bombing in London, and that Saturday there seemed to be an enhanced sense of nervousness and anxiety. Since the declaration of war a year earlier, it had been a time characterised by an unusual mix of high adrenaline, and mundane tasks. A year of Barrage Balloons, black outs, gas masks, ration books and air raid sirens, interspersed with fire drills, taped windows and sandbag protection. But that morning Ted had the uneasy feeling that the war was about to enter into a new phase, and old Jack, the Boer War veteran, was in full agreement. It had been Jack who had forecast the war two years before. While everyone else felt that the politicians would surely not be stupid enough to start another war, Jack had been steadfast in his judgement that World War Two was coming.

Now as they stood there together at the garden fence, the two of them drinking deeply from their steaming mugs, how Ted wished that Jack had been wrong. As a result of Jack's correct prophesy, Ted's son Tom was now far away, serving in the Middle East, a constant source of worry for both him and his wife Elsie. As Rita gathered some eggs from the pen, Ted drained his mug and set back to work, burying the shelter in eighteen inches of soil. A shout from the house indicated that Elsie had arrived back from the butchers, and Rita rushed in to see what meat her mum had managed to purchase. Over another cup of tea, Elsie and her daughter sorted out the rations: 4 ounces of bacon, 4 ounces of ham, a small portion of lamb, 8 ounces of butter, packet of tea, the National Loaf, fish and sausages, each item stored with careful attention. The chicken and ducks at the end of the garden provided a useful supplement to the food store, in the form of extra meat and eggs. Also a large part of the garden had been given over to growing vegetables, meaning there was always a plentiful supply of onions, carrots, marrows, potatoes, runner beans, tomatoes and lettuces. Ted and his friend Harry Carter also shared a large allotment in Weavers Fields at the end of the lane, and from this they could trade with neighbours, and occasionally sell produce from a market stall in Brick Lane.

Ted was now protecting the entrance to the shelter by creating an earth embankment, and positioning a steel shield, all the while continuing to listen to Jack's good intentioned advice. Elsie came out to see how Ted was progressing. Having first met in their schooldays, they had married at the end of World War One, and their affection was still plain for all to see. Like most people in the East End, their lives could be difficult, and they had their rows, but they were well aware that deprivation was relative, knowing that there were people in the lane who were far worse off than them. Both Elsie and Rita cycled to Great Eastern Street every weekday, being lucky enough to have regular work in a factory making army uniforms, while Ted and Harry Carter worked the coal lorries in the winter. This revenue was supplemented by Ted's sideline of shoe mending, as by using leather off cuts gathered from the market and old tyre dumps, he found he could make a steady profit prolonging the life of the district's footwear. The added income he earned from his allotment, plus his newly acquired air raid duties, ensured the family did ok considering the limitations of their situation.

As Elsie and Ted shared a Woodbine cigarette, there was a sudden clucking and flapping from the poultry at the end of the garden as the 11.05am from Liverpool Street to Chelmsford passed over the arches. After five minutes of old Jack saying how he could improve Ted's shelter, he then sheepishly asked if Ted could spare five minutes to drain his one. Ted and Elsie exchanged knowing glances before Ted vaulted over the fence, it was the least they could do for a good long standing neighbour, who had just recently been bereaved by the loss of his wife Joan.

Winston Churchill walked briskly through the quadrangle of the Foreign Office, accompanied by his bodyguard, Detective Inspector Walter Thompson. Turning left into King Charles Street, they entered a large civil service building surrounded by sandbags. Before entering the meeting room, Churchill made a brief phone call to his wife Clementine at Chequers, the weekend retreat for all Prime Ministers. After informing her that he intended to arrive there that evening, he replaced the phone and poured himself a whiskey and soda. As Churchill entered the meeting room, the assembled persons present hushed their conversations, and turned attentively to their leader. They were there to discuss the German invasion strategy, known as 'Operation Sea Lion' a plan that was put together by the Germans, in the immediate aftermath and euphoria of the French surrender. On planning to invade across the narrow strip of channel, the Germans soon realised that the practicalities of such an invasion revealed it to be an exceptionally bold and daring undertaking. Though the channel was narrow, they realised there could be no element of surprise, plus the British Navy dominated the sea area in which they must operate. They came to the conclusion that there could be no possible attempt of an invasion, without the prerequisite of complete mastery of the air.

To a military strategist like Churchill, who was steeped in British History, the tides, currents and weather considerations, needing to be taken into account in a channel invasion, were plainly an advantage to Britain's defences. Added to the German's problem with air cover, Churchill and his Generals could obviously see Hitler's dilemma with his operation. As Winston Churchill sat down at the oval table, he looked at the faces turned towards him, scanning each individual for signs of weakness.

To his left was a frail looking man with a sickly pallor, but his eyes were bright and defiant. This was the deposed appeaser, Conservative

Prime Minister Neville Chamberlain, who in the interests of national unity, Churchill had allocated a place in the war cabinet. Next to him sat a small neat man of earnest expression, this was the leader of the Labour Party, Clement Atlee. To Churchill he was a man of war experience, pragmatic and sensible, someone with whom he could easily work. Along from him was Lord Halifax, a tall gaunt Conservative with a withered arm. Churchill recognised in him a shrewdness in dealing with bullshit, while always getting to the real issues. Alongside him was Labour politician Arthur Greenwood, someone who Churchill valued as a wise counsellor of high courage, and a good and helpful friend. And so it went on, Anthony Eden, a Conservative, Sir Archibald Sinclair, a Liberal, A V Alexander, Labour, men from all the political parties, resolute and defiant, channeling their talents for the national interest.

They in turn observed their leader, for Churchill had the capacity to both irritate and infuriate, but they also recognised in him his courageous determination, and capacity to inspire. Churchill took another swig of his whiskey, and lit up his second Havana of the day before addressing the War Cabinet. He started by asking Lord Beaverbrooke, who was Minister for Air Production, the present state of affairs as regards aircraft numbers. Beaverbrooke had some good news to report, telling Churchill that from June to August that year they had produced and repaired 4,575 aircraft, including 875 Hurricanes and Spitfires. This news was of vital importance as regards Britain's ability to defend its shores, and Churchill was heartily encouraged. His strategy of using Labour politicians like Mr Herbert Morrison, as Minister of Supply, and Mr Ernest Bevin, as Minister of

Labour, had seemed to bring the Trade Unions on side with their employers, and the result was now a massive working together for the nation in arms. The pink, plump and rounded features of Churchill positively beamed, as he prepared to give those assembled, his evaluation of the situation as it stood.

After a deep draw on his cigar he growled 'Our fate now depends upon victory in the air, I believe the German leaders have recognised that all their plans for the invasion of Britain depend on winning air supremacy above the Channel and the chosen landing places on our south coast. At the moment whenever the weather is favorable, waves of German bombers, protected by fighters, surge over this island in an effort to destroy our airfields and military installations in daylight, and in this objective they have had some limited success. If these attacks continue with the same intensity in the coming month, there is a real threat that it will severely limit our ability to engage with the enemy in our own airspace. Therefore, we must continue to strain every sinew to prevent this eventuality. However, I am pleased to report that these attacks at present are met by our fighter squadrons, and in most cases repelled and broken up. Up to now their losses are averaging three to one in our favour, and it has cost them very dear. As things stand, it would be a very hazardous undertaking for the Germans to attempt to activate Operation Sea Lion. Nevertheless our intelligence sources tell us that their preparations for invasion on a great scale are going forward, and if this invasion is going to be tried at all it does not seem that it can be long delayed. The weather may break at any time. Besides this, it is difficult for the enemy to keep these gatherings of ships waiting about indefinitely while they are bombed every night by our bombers.

Therefore, we must regard the next week or so as a very important period in our history.'

There was an initial silence in the room as Churchill ceased his address, almost immediately followed by a scraping of chairs and a round of applause. The heartening news of the RAF pilots success, plus the impressive manufacturing figures regarding aircraft, had boosted the mood of patriotic defiance. After some further questions on strategic defence issues, the meeting was eventually broken up by Churchill declaring that no army can march on an empty stomach, and suggesting lunch would be a good idea.

It had taken Ted Harrison up to an hour to drain and repair old Jack Walker's Anderson Shelter, before being able to return to Elsie and Rita in their small kitchen and enjoy a bacon sandwich, washed down with a mug of tea. They were eventually joined by Harry's wife Joyce, who lived four doors away. They had all known each other from childhood, having all gone to the Globe Road Primary School. As Joyce gratefully accepted an offer of a cup of tea, Ted could not help thinking how Joyce and Harry were so similar in temperament. Both relentlessly cheerful, he imagined they must have their down days, but to date he had never seen them displayed. After Joyce had mentioned that Harry was working on the allotment, Ted slipped on his jacket and said he would pay him a visit. Elsie and Joyce exchanged knowing glances, before shouting after him not to be too long in the pub.

As he strolled down the lane towards Weavers Fields, Ted looked up at the blue sky. It was a fine day, a day that would be perfect for bombers. He and Harry had chosen to join the ARP instead of the Home Guard at this stage of the hostilities, mainly because they felt that they could be of more use to the community in which they lived. After their experiences as frontline soldiers in World War One, they had felt that the Home Guard, without being disrespectful to those who recruited, was mainly at this stage a Government initiative to keep people busy and feel less helpless. They had both made a pact that if the worse happened and the country was invaded, there would be no doubt in their minds that they would fight to the death to defend the island.

After making the decision to join the ARP, they had both recruited on the same day at Bethnal Green Town Hall, which was the nearest ARP control centre. Their local wardens post was in their old school, Globe Road Primary, and they had to report there on most evenings. The duties this entailed were numerous, from informing medical and rescue services of any incidents, to rendering first aid, investigating unexploded bombs, ensuring blackout regulations, and informing the locals the whereabouts of shelters and homeless centers. So far there had been countless air raid warnings without too much bombing, but as Ted looked up at the clear sky that morning, the nagging anxiety that he had felt all morning intensified.

Nearing the end of the lane he was joined by a small scruffy individual who excitedly jumped from one foot to the other. This was little Sid, one of the more unfortunate inhabitants of Three Colts Lane. Orphaned at an early age, and now in his mid thirties, he was still childlike in his demeanour. He now lived alone in a dark dingy dwelling at the eastern end of the lane, in a house that had originally belonged to his parents. He somehow scraped a living doing street cleaning and park keeping duties. Ted occasionally gave him work delivering the allotment vegetables, and helping to set up Ted and Harry's stall in the market. It was small change, but it made Sid feel useful and valued, even more so because he looked up to Ted and Harry as heroic war heroes. He admired them to such an extent that he had joined the ARP as one of their part time assistants. Sid persisted with the usual enquiries whenever he saw Ted or Harry, 'When are they going to invade Ted?' 'They won't know what's hit them will they Ted?' 'We will give them hell won't we Ted?' Ted quietly nodded his agreement, as Sid hung on his every word and tried to imitate Ted's walk.

As Weavers Fields came into their view, they could see Harry crouched over some prize sized marrows. On hearing them approaching, Harry turned and waved a cheerful greeting. The spread of vegetables on display was impressive, with Harry being particularly proud of his tomato crop. Harry Carter was always competitive in everything he did, and he always liked to get one over his best friend Ted. After asking Sid to load some of the veg in boxes, he invited Ted back to his house to see the latest enhancements to his Anderson Shelter. Upon entering the garden, Harry presented his shelter with a flourish. Harry had built up the doorway with sandbags to form a porch, giving the structure a more homely appearance. Proudly inviting Ted inside, he had painted the walls with whitewash, and rigged up a battery wireless set on some assembled shelves. On the floor were some canvas hammocks, a Tilley lamp for light, and a Valor paraffin stove for warmth. Ted remarked that it was more comfortable than the house, to which Harry replied 'That's the idea'. They left the house for the short walk to the Duke of Wellington Pub, a regular ritual they had indulged for many a year.

Winston Churchill leaned back in his chair and sipped a glass of his favourite Pol Roger champagne, a lighted cigar in his other hand. He had enjoyed a meal of smoked salmon, mushroom pâté and chicken. He had returned from the meeting at Whitehall, in order to have lunch at Downing Street, accompanied by two of his colleagues from the War Cabinet: Arthur Greenwood and Archibald Sinclair.

Now as the catering staff cleared their plates, the three men engaged in more serious conversation on the direction of the war. The Minister for Air, Archie Sinclair was explaining why to date, the RAF had seemed to have the advantage over the Lufwaffe. By having to protect their bombers, the German fighter planes had to fly at 20,000ft or below, this left them vulnerable to the superior manoeuverability, and concentrated firepower of the Spitfires, plus the German's distance from base meant their operational time was severely limited. Churchill opinioned that the German high command had seriously underestimated Britain's aircraft numbers and pilot skill, deducing that there seemed to be a lack of German unity among their top Generals in their invasion strategy.

They went on to discuss the possibility of more intense bombing of London – after all, the capital was the seat of British Government. London was the capital of the British Empire, housing the great buildings that played an important part in England's great history with structures that were etched deeply in the psyche of the nation: like Buckingham Palace, Westminster Palace, St Paul's Cathedral and the Tower of London. Destruction of these much cherished landmarks, would deal an enormous blow to the morale of the people. Churchill voiced concern as regards night attacks, as the radar system was not yet perfected, and night fighter planes like the Blenheims and Defiants were still in their trial period. Archibald Sinclair informed Churchill that more anti aircraft guns were being stationed on the south coast, and would be crucial as the first line of defence in the event of such attacks. Finally rising from his chair, Churchill thanked his friends and retired to his chambers for his customary afternoon nap.

The Duke of Wellington was a fine example of all the typical east end pubs that existed on practically every corner street. These establishments were essential meeting places for the small knit communities, and the smell of stale tobacco and spilt ale, accompanied by the sound of indifferent piano playing, was the common ambience. The Duke was enjoying it's usual good trade, as Ted and Harry pushed through the door and entered the smoke filled atmosphere. The two of them were popular and much respected in the local environs, consequently they had to turn down several invitations to join gathered groups on their way to the bar. Though sociable, they preferred to keep their counsel within each other's company when drinking. The ruddy, cheery countenance of the landlord Henry Harrington, was there to greet them, and he was already pouring two pints of stout and mild, their usual liquid refreshment. As Henry handed them their pints he advised 'Drink em down quick lads, now that Winnie's bombed Berlin it won't be long before London is a pile of rubble'. Harry smiled as he savoured the first swallow of the frothy fluid, while Ted nodded and handed him one shilling and four pennies.

Henry was referring to the minor bombing raid on Berlin a week or so before, which was ordered by Churchill in an attempt to show defiance. Harry let the beer hit the pit of his stomach before replying

'Get your retaliation in first, it's always a good tactic'. Henry laughed and said 'Adolf won't like it, he will be very annoyed'. Harry sharply retorted 'Good'. Henry smiled and moved up the bar to serve someone else. Both Ted and Harry had been unhappy with the weak leadership of Chamberlain, now at last the country had a leader who understood that wars are won by fighting. Recognising that if the Nazi war machine was not resisted, it would devour everyone in it's path, they realised that there really was no alternative.

They would have wished for it to be different, for deep in the recesses of their minds they still carried the devastating memories of Flanders. They remembered all too well the chilling fear of death, the blood and the mud, and the sudden brutal loss of brothers in arms. When Churchill spoke on the radio they were captivated, his speeches being delivered in a voice for the entire nation, somehow combining grandiose and democratic. His words released in them that deep chord of patriotism, peculiar to an island race. That indefinable sense of knowing what it meant to be British. His patriotism inspired them to believe that Britain's way of life needed to be defended passionately, and ultimately was worth the supreme sacrifice. After draining their first pints swiftly, Harry ordered two more, as Ted offered him a Woodbine cigarette from a tobacco tin he kept tucked away in his pocket. Though complete opposites in looks and personality, the two men had bonded securely in shared experience. Ted was short and dark, quiet, thoughtful and serious, while Harry was tallish and fair, cheerful and more volatile. From an early age they had attended the same schools, and played in the same streets. As patriotic young men, they had shared the same horrific experiences in Flanders, before marrying their child sweethearts on their return from the conflict. As striving married men with young families, they had both worked and played together. Be it shared holidays hop picking in Yalding, Kent, or visiting White Hart Lane to see Tottenham Hotspur, they were invariably always together. And now with Britain on the point of invasion, they were inevitably facing the menace side by side.

Standing at the bar engrossed in their conversation, they were suddenly interrupted when someone pushed through the crowd and tapped Harry on the shoulder. They turned to see the familiar face of Jimmy Mills, shouting to make himself heard above the piano playing in the corner. Jimmy was one of their ARP team stationed at Globe Road Primary School, and he was confirming the time of 6.30pm for their duties that evening. After having the time confirmed, Jimmy nodded towards the end of the bar and said 'Have you seen who is standing over there?' On the other side of the bar two men were talking in an animated manner. Sticking out of their jacket pockets clear for all to see, were copies of the *Daily Worker*, a left wing Communist Paper. Charlie Smithers and Ronnie Silver made no secret of the fact that they thought a German invasion would be a good thing for Britain, and in particular the working classes. Ted and Harry were well aware that there were people who had some sympathy with that viewpoint, and they certainly knew the views of Smithers and Silver, but they had no time for such twisted ideological thinking. When they looked at people like them, they felt nothing but contempt, and dismissed them as cowardly traitors. Ted noticed that Harry was glaring across at them, and knowing that look all too well, he quickly bought two more stout and milds, and told Harry to cool it.

Winston Churchill was abruptly awakened from his afternoon slumbers, by the shrill ring of the telephone. The voice on the other end of the line was the Secretary of State for War, Anthony Eden, and he was phoning from the Cabinet War Rooms. He informed Churchill that the Observer Corps on the south coast, had reported increased enemy aircraft activity over the channel. Churchill looked at the large oak grandfather clock at the end of his bed, the solid metal hands pointed to 3.30pm. After informing Eden that he would make his way across to the Cabinet War Rooms immediately, he quickly phoned his wife Clementine to say that there could be some delay in his arrival at Chequers. The Cabinet War Rooms existed deep underneath the Whitehall Building's that existed between King Charles Street and Parliament Square. They covered an area of more than 3 acres, and could accommodate more than 500 people if necessary.

In the sub basement there was a canteen, a small hospital, and a shooting range. On the floor above these existed a warren of rooms used as sleeping quarters, totally devoid of outside light, with ceilings so low occupants could not stand upright. Adjacent to these rooms was the sound proof cabinet room, and it was here that Winston Churchill entered to find the entire War Cabinet seated around a cloth covered table.

Taking a seat at the table, Churchill was informed by the Minister for Air, Sir Archibald Sinclair, that the increasing intensity of the dog fights over the south coast, seemed to suggest that they were part of a bigger operation. He went on to say that by increasing the waves of attacks, the Luftwaffe hoped to engage and destroy more Spitfires and

Hurricanes, in the hope that their bombers could destroy our undefended airfields, communications and installations.

Winston Churchill looked grave, leaning back in his seat he gave a grimace, before growling 'We know the enemy have ample aircraft numbers to send out new waves of attacks. Because our squadrons have to refuel after 80 minutes, or rearm after a five minute engagement, a fresh wave of unchallenged German squadrons could prove disastrous. It must therefore be one of our principle objectives, to direct our squadrons to not have too many planes on the ground refueling or rearming at any one time. Meanwhile let us hope and pray that our brave pilots excel, and that the Luftwaffe fail miserably in their mission to destroy our air force'.

The War Cabinet then rose from the table to assemble in the Operations Room, in the centre of which was a large scale map table. Standing around it were about 20 highly trained men and women, surrounded by their telephone assistants and a battery of telephones, coloured black, red, white and green. On the walls were an assortment of maps and graphs, with which it was possible to use coloured marker pins, and coordinate information from the chiefs of staff for the War Cabinet. Around the map table, the men and women, acting on the information from the Observer Corps, pushed discs around the table indicating the movements of British and German aircraft. Thousands of messages were coming in on the colourful array of telephones, all communicated by portable sets held by the Observer Corps, via the numerous headquarters of Fighter Command.

The War Cabinet observed as an attack of 40 plus enemy aircraft were reported to be coming in from the German stations in the Dieppe area, this was swiftly followed by 60 plus. It was obvious that a serious battle impended. On the table before them, the discs being pushed around the table increased in volume. The sky over the south coast must have been a swarm of fighters and bombers, creating a battle that looked to have generated 100 plus individual dogfights. Winston Churchill found himself tensing with excitement, as reports came in of successful strikes against enemy bombers. After 30 minutes of intense fighting, most of the RAF squadrons had descended to refuel. Churchill looked anxiously at the map table, another wave of 40 plus enemy aircraft at this time would be a disaster. To his relief the shifting of the discs showed a continuous eastward movement of German bombers and fighters, it appeared the enemy were going home.

The release of tension in the room was tangible, as several members of the Cabinet congratulated themselves.

Unbeknown to them at that very moment, V shaped blips of light were appearing on the convex glass screens of the coastal radar stations. Suddenly the emergency red phone shrilled loudly in the Cabinet War Rooms. The message that was conveyed made the blood run cold.

Two hundred German bombers accompanied by fighters, had been spotted over the channel approaching the south coast. Winston Churchill immediately went into conference with Clement Atlee and Archibald Sinclair. The RAF had literally minutes to get every squadron airborn to engage the enemy. It was an impossible task. Feeling utterly powerless, Churchill watched the discs on the table being shifted closer to the vulnerable airfields and installations. For the first time since the hostilities began he felt a momentary sense of despair, the odds were great, the stakes infinite. But incredibly, the discs were being pushed in an increasingly north westerly direction, the airfields were not the target. In the room there was an initial wave of relief, followed swiftly by a soaring surge of adrenaline. The Bombers were heading for London.

As Ted Harrison leaned back in his tin bath, he could hear the voices of Elsie and Rita in the garden. They were chatting with Joyce and Harry, and their three daughters, Violet, Vera and Bessie. The three daughters had all just dropped in for a cup of tea, after returning from Roman Road Market. Ted and Harry had left the Duke of Wellington pub an hour earlier, and returned to Ted's house together, as Harry's wife Joyce made it a habit to spend Saturday afternoons at Ted and Elsie's.

While they were all out in the garden making the most of the fine late summers day, Ted had boiled several pots of water to half fill his tin bath. Having placed the bath in his small scullery, he was now languishing in the warm water, drifting in and out of a light sleep. As he dozed he heard Harry's oldest daughter Violet, as she said goodbye to the others and left by the side gate. She was the only one of the daughters who lived away from Three Colts Lane, having got married and moved to a house in Stepney Green. Her young husband had been posted overseas soon after the wedding, so she spent a lot of her time back home socialising with her sisters.

Ted could vaguely hear the sound of Harry talking about the London bombings in World War One, and it sounded like they had been joined in the conversation by old Jack Walker across the garden fence. Ted knew that Harry had reason to be bitter about those bombings, as he had lost a neice and nephew when their school in Poplar had received a direct hit. Ted was interrupted in his semi conscious reverie by his wife shouting from the garden, 'Ted, how long you going to be? We want to put the kettle on' Ted replied 'Won't be a jiffy' and rose carefully from the now lukewarm water. Outside in the garden, Elsie and Joyce were listening to Vera and Bessie describing some Hollywood film they had recently seen at a picture palace in Mile End. Meanwhile Harry and old Jack were talking about the fine vegetable crop that Ted had managed to cultivate in his garden that summer. It was just as Jack was admiring Ted's fine crop of lettuces, that Harry suddenly thought he could detect the faint sound of a distant air raid siren. Looking instinctively up into the vast blue sky, Harry could just make out what looked like a massive swarm of tiny bees on the southerly horizon. Everyone in the garden looked, as Harry excitedly pointed towards the extraordinary sight. In the kitchen Ted could hear Harry's agitated alarm, and still not fully dressed, rushed into the garden to see the cause of the commotion. By now there was not just one faint siren, but a series, as the undulating wailing note was taken up by district after district. Looking to the skies, the small black dots that Harry had originally set his eyes on, could now be defined as hundreds of aircraft of differing shapes and sizes. A huge phalanx of German planes were now droning on a westerly course up the River Thames, before banking in majestic orderliness, in the direction of the East End Docks. The sky was now full of Heinkel bombers, being closely escorted by Messerscmitt 109 fighters, but with no sign of the RAF. As everyone in the garden stood in awe at this riveting scene, old Jack Walker was the first to find his voice.

'Blimey, we've lost the war, where's our boys?' They were all suddenly galvanized into action when the Bethnal Green siren activated, spreading it's message of alarm, and setting the pulses racing. Harry sprinted back to his dwelling to get his tin hat, whistle and gas masks, while Ted and Elsie rushed back into the house to get some blankets and tea making facilities for the Anderson shelter. In the last year it was a routine they had experienced countless times, but never before with such feelings of fear and trepidation. Elsie, Rita, Joyce, Vera and Bessie, were soon ensconced in Ted's shelter, and as Harry swiftly returned from his house with some valued personal possessions, they heard the first distant dull thudding explosions in the docklands area.

Meanwhile back in his kitchen, Ted had donned his white tin hat marked W, and was now reaching for a Peek Frean biscuit tin under the sink. Going outside to the shelter he handed the tin to Elsie, inside it were their small savings and ready cash. After Harry had checked with old Jack that he was comfortable in his own shelter, both Harry and Ted said their goodbyes, and hurried towards their ARP post in Globe Road.

At the eastern end of Three Colts Lane they bumped into Little Sid, cowering in his doorway. Sid's eyes were like saucers, and his lips twitched with alarm as he asked 'Have we been invaded?' Harry typically used a football analogy as he answered 'No chance Sid, this is our Cup Final, and we have the advantage of playing at home'. Ted asked Sid if he was coming to the ARP post. Sid hesitated for a moment, before retreating into his house, only to reappear almost immediately wearing his tin hat slightly askew.

As they crossed Cambridge Heath Road, hundreds of people were heading in the direction of Victoria Park. In the park was an enormous communal shelter, and though the interior was damp and dingy, it was capable of housing up to 1500 people. Up above their heads Ted, Harry and Sid, could hear the constant throbbing of aircraft, as the increasingly frequent explosions erupted within their earshot. In Bethnal Green Gardens, the RAF Balloon Command were busily winching up a Barrage Balloon from a stationary wagon. Some people were forcing their way down the steps of Bethnal Green Tube Station, as various officials struggled with the crowds. By the time Ted, Harry and Sid had turned into Globe Road, enormous mushrooms of smoke were rising in the sky above the dockland area. Just as they were entering the school building, Harry punched the air and exclaimed 'Go get 'em boys' as a cluster of Spitfires and Hurricanes sped over their heads.

Once inside the school, they were met by Jimmy Mills, and their ARP station leader Arthur Turnbull. Middle class, officious and arrogant, Arthur Turnbull had not made himself very popular in the Bethnal Green area in the time he had resided there. Chosen to head control of the Globe Road Station, by the ARP High Command, he was very much an outsider, and obviously not of East End stock. Harry and Jimmy had both clashed with him on several issues, and even Ted had on occasions bitten his lip to avoid confrontation. Arthur looked stern and annoyed as he remonstrated 'You lot have taken your time' before Harry had a chance to answer, Arthur went on 'Looks like we are down to five as Johnny has cried off. Been told he took one look out the window and didn't fancy it – still it's better to find out now'.

Johnny Briggs lived in the Old Ford Road, and was the final member of their local ARP team. Both Ted and Harry were surprised to hear this news about Johnny, but as they knew from their experiences in World War One, you could never tell how people were going to react under fire. The radio set began to crackle, and a faint voice could be heard. Arthur Turnbull tuned in to the incoming message, his face a picture of determined concentration as he absorbed the information. At the end of the call he turned to Ted, Harry, Sid and Jimmy 'Looks like we are going to have to spread ourselves a bit thin lads. Need a volunteer for the Bow Road area, seems there's a bit of panic after an explosion'. Sid seemed to move behind Harry, as Ted put himself forward for the assignment. Soon Ted was outside making his way south to the Mile End Road, ahead of him the sun seemed to be setting in the east, as a huge orange glow flickered above the docks. Keeping close to the buildings, he made his way through the hurrying crowds, the ringing of fire engines beginning to dominate his senses. As he entered Mile End Road, he looked up to see a Messerscmitt 109 swerve at about 20,000ft, to avoid a swooping Spitfire. Struggling to comprehend the compulsive reality of what he was witnessing, he instinctively crouched down, before heading off in the direction of Bow Road.

To the west in the Cabinet War Rooms, there was a hive of activity. Hundreds of staff and secretaries were processing information and typing huge directives, as the telephones rang continuously. Meanwhile the War Cabinet were transfixed in the map room, as the discs on the table informed them of the duel between the RAF and the Luftwaffe as it unfolded.

Standing next to Churchill was a tall man of upright military bearing, this was the Chief Commander of the Home Forces, General Alan Brooke. He was in charge of the Home defence policy, in the event of Germany activating Operation Sea lion. Commander Brooke was discussing with Churchill the German tactic of dropping hundreds of incendiary bombs, and the possible significance. As a result of this discourse, Winston Churchill summoned a meeting of the War Cabinet. Back inside the sound proof Cabinet Room, the members of the War Cabinet took their seats, their faces taut with tension and responsibility. The room was brightly lit with artificial strip lighting, illuminating the metal pipes that generously adorned the walls, making the room feel cool and damp. The Cabinet looked towards Churchill through a great fog of smoke, as a combination of cigarettes, Attlee's pipe and Churchill's cigar, polluted the atmospheare. Winston Churchill began his assessment of the situation.

'Pray gentlemen, it appears we are entering into a new phase of the war, I suspect that the fires presently being ignited in the East End docks are a prelude to further night time bombing, as they will provide an excellent guide to their targets in darkness. At present it is too early to judge whether the Germans are attempting to paralyse London's shipping capability, or this is just the prelude to a much bigger operation. Therefore, we will need to keep up the utmost vigilance on our coastlines, and prepare ourselves for the worst'. After some further discussions on operational procedures, Churchill concluded the meeting and left the room.

Before returning to the map room, Churchill retreated to a small dingy chamber off the corridor. The room was austerely furnished with just a bed and a small writing desk, with a tiny anteroom leading off to the side. It was here that Churchill could make his transatlantic phone calls to President Roosevelt of America, and after closing the door, he proceeded to update the President on the current situation. After some fifteen minutes, Churchill emerged to be confronted by his bodyguard, Walter Thompson. He had known and been protected by

Thompson for many years, and he liked and trusted him implicitly. Thompson suggested to Churchill that it would be advisable for his wife and his youngest daughter Mary, to be moved from Chequers, as German Intelligence would be well aware of it being the weekend residence of the Prime Minister. Thompson explained to him that on such a clear night, Chequers would be an easy target for the bombers with its easily visible drive. Churchill was persuaded, and arranged for Clementine to be moved to Ditchley Park in Oxfordshire, home of his friend, Conservative MP Ronald Tree. Once this arrangement was finalised, Winston Churchill returned to the map room, his body language bristling with defiance.

As Ted reached his destination in Bow Road, he could see crowds of people milling around in aimless confusion.

In the line of buildings to his right, there was a large gap where there was once a building. In its place was a massive pile of rubble, and this was where fireman and ambulance crew were congregated. It looked as if the firefighters had just completed their task, and the medical men were pulling some bodies out of the ruin. Ted spotted a member of the Auxilary Fire Service, who was standing next to a taxi with a water pump in tow, his face blackened by smoke. Ted shouted above the aircraft noise to make himself heard 'I am from the ARP post in Bethnal Green, what do you want me to do?' The man shook his hand and replied 'Well for a start you can get all these people away from here and into shelters.' Ted looked around at some of the faces of the people. Many of them appeared dazed and bewildered, others seemed to be displaying bold truculence, and adamantly refusing to go underground.

Eventually Ted was joined by another ARP Warden, and together they managed to direct and persuade the bulk of the people to attend the communal shelter in Mile End Park. Some of the people shouted to Ted 'What about the poor sods in the church' Acting on this enquiry, Ted walked swiftly towards the eastern end of Bow Road, the sky to his right was displaying a vivid scorching red, and the sound of distant explosions were now a constant backdrop. On entering Bow Church, Ted was confronted by the sight of about 100 people kneeling in the crypt, many of them were crying as they prayed. Ted quickly surmised that there was nothing he could do to move these devoted reverent souls, and hurriedly left the church.

It was about 6.45pm and night was falling when Ted finally arrived back at Globe Road School, the consistent wail of the All Clear siren had sounded as he was heading back to his post. The post was being manned by Jimmy, and already there were homeless people arriving at the school from docklands, carrying a few snatched belongings, accompanied by family pets. These people were being looked after by the Salvation Army, and to Ted and Jimmy, they presented a sad sight. After handing Ted a woodbine cigarette, Jimmy quickly informed him that Harry and King Arthur, his ironic title for Turnbull, had been called out to an explosion in the Whitechapel Road. He then went on to enquire 'Have you heard about Silvertown?' Ted drew gratefully on the woodbine before shaking his head. Jimmy eagerly went on 'Totally cut off, hemmed in on all sides by 100 foot flames. Rescue services can't get near it'.

Jimmy was interrupted by the return of Arthur and Harry, their clothing coated in thick black dust. Arthur looked grim as he said 'I think we are in for a long night lads, don't for a moment think that's it for the evening'. Harry looked across at Ted and informed him 'Clarke's shoe factory in the Whitechapel Road has gone completely up in smoke, not to mention the spice works'. Ted grimaced and shook his head, before asking 'Where's Sid?' Arthur gave a disdainful snort before saying 'Gone AWOL. What did you expect? He was about as much use as a dustpan and brush in an earthquake'. Ted and Harry smiled to each other in spite of themselves, for they knew Sid only too well, and were not surprised to hear of his desertion. Arthur went on 'You have got half an hour to check things back home lads, then report back here pronto.' Ted and Harry needed no encouragement to depart immediately, and were soon making their way through the dark, smoke ridden streets. Towards the docklands they could see the sky ablaze, and hear the fierce crackling of the fires, while all the time, the harsh acrid smell of cordite pervaded their nostrils. On reaching the top of Three Colts Lane they were both relieved to see there was no obvious damage to the landscape as they approached Ted's house. Once inside, they found everyone assembled in the kitchen. Elsie, looking both pleased and relieved to see them quipped, 'You must have smelt the teapot'. They then swapped stories of their experiences in the recent raid, while refreshing themselves with a quick sandwich and a cup of tea.

Soon after the All Clear siren had sounded, Winston Churchill, accompanied by Clement Atlee and Arthur Greenwood, had been driven to the Imperial Chemical building on the Embankment, in order to see the extent of the fires. From the high stone balconies at the top of the building, there was a panoramic view of the River Thames. To their left it was possible to see that the greater part of docklands was in flames, and, as a consequence, would provide a perfect beacon for night time bombers. Upon returning to the Cabinet War Rooms, Churchill summoned General Pile, commander of the Air Defence Artillery.

On arrival at the War Cabinet Rooms, General Pile was shown into the Cabinet Room where the War Cabinet, plus General Alan Brooke, were seated in various informal groups. Winston Churchill invited Pile to sit down and offered him a cigar, before asking him, 'General Pile, how many of our anti-aircraft guns are presently in position to respond to a major air attack in London?' General Pile thought carefully before answering. He knew from experience that when Churchill asked a question, accuracy in detail was expected. The genial countenance of Pile looked slightly perturbed as he declined the offer of a cigar, before replying, 'Just 92'. There was an intake of breath around the table before Pile swiftly added, 'The reason the number is so small is because we have dispersed our artillery to other provincial cities and coastlines.' Churchill pursed his lips and drew on his Havana. He had the utmost regard for General Pile's abilities, and was confident in setting him a challenge. Churchill paused briefly before explaining his requirement. 'We believe that London is now most likely to be the main focus of night time air attacks, and that it is of the utmost urgency to get those guns back in London within 48 hours. Can you do it?' Again General Pile hesitated slightly before answering.

'If it is humanly possible it will be done.' Churchill smiled and replied 'Right answer.' He then concluded the meeting by resignedly stating, 'In the meantime, London's nocturnal defences are in the hands of six squadrons of Blenheims and Defiants.' It was soon after this meeting that Churchill returned to the map room. Horrific reports were coming back from the firefighters at docklands regarding lack of water – the Germans having shrewdly chosen to attack when the Thames was at low tide. Suddenly the red phone on the desk shrilled it's intimidating alarm – the news was not good.

Over a hundred German Junkers were approaching the south coast, and at the same time there were reports of a concentration of barges both on the Channel, and at the Dutch port of Rotterdam. On receiving this news, Churchill's veins flooded with adrenaline, this combination of air and sea activity could mean only one thing, 'Operation Sea Lion' was possibly underway. The War Cabinet immediately authorised General Alan Brooke to issue the codeword 'Cromwell' signifying Alert No 1, 'Invasion imminent and probable within 12 hours'. From Fowey in Cornwall to Dover in Kent, half a million members of the Home Guard were alerted for the first invasion in more than a century. Sophisticated preparations were in place to turn the southern coastline into a raging caudron of fire, at the first sign of a German landing. Waiting further inland was an invisible army of 5,000 men, highly trained in guerilla warfare, and courtesy of the United States, equipped with the latest cutting edge weaponry. The Junkers meanwhile droned relentlessly to their planned destination, their targets illuminated by the huge rolling fire that was blazing on the Thames.

After reporting back on time to the ARP post, Ted and Harry had found the queues of homeless people from docklands massively increased. Arthur Turnbull was on his radio set, getting reports that the fires were now so intense in Wapping and the surrounding areas, that fighting the flames with water was pointless. Turnbull immediately instructed Ted, Jimmy and Harry to patrol Mile End and Whitechapel, in order to intercept and direct the disorientated people emerging from docklands. After agreeing to split up from the others, Ted was now heading down the Whitechapel Road, holding his specially shaded torch in front of him. He was approached out of the gloom by one poor family carrying their salvaged belongings in a handcart, needing little encouragement to describe to him the horrific scenes down on the Thames. After Ted had directed them to Globe Road, there were others to tell him the same stories. Tales of burning barges drifting everywhere, dense smoke, flames blazing furiously, all the time accompanied by the deafening roar of burning wood.

It was just as he was engaged in one of these conversations, that the first distant waves of the air raid siren began to echo it's dreaded alarm. They had been instructed by Arthur Turnbull to return immediately to the ARP post in the event of an air raid. The hundreds of homeless people at the school needed to be directed to the shelters, as it was not good practice to have too many people congregated in one place at such a perilous time. By the time Ted had turned into Globe Road, he could hear the heavy uneven throb of the approaching enemy Bombers. Outside the ARP post, Arthur Turnbull was already attempting to guide the crowds towards the Victoria Park shelter. On seeing Ted, Turnbull immediately called for assistance, as more people appeared on the streets running in all directions.

It was just at the point when Jimmy and Harry returned to the post, that they all heard the distinctive clatter of incendiaries on the roofs and pavements. Ted and Arthur, acted as one, as they immediately headed for the buckets of sand that were stacked against the school wall. Eventually joined by Harry and Jimmy, they all spent the next hour continually stifling the small fires that were erupting, as the bells of the fire engines sounded their constant alarm. At one stage Jimmy looked towards the skyline in the south, the whole horizon was an unbroken cycle of flames. Turning to the others he shouted, 'The bloody world's on fire!' Harry, never short of a reply, answered smartly, 'Welcome to hell.' All the while the explosions seemed to be erupting in much closer proximity, shaking the ground and deafening the eardrums.

Meanwhile – back in Ted's Anderson shelter – Elsie, Rita, Joyce, Vera and Bessie, huddled together anxiously, while overhead the Bombers circled like dogs trying to pick up a scent.

Back at the Cabinet War Rooms, there was the gradual realisation with each hour of the bombing raid, that Operation Sea Lion had not been activated. As the lookouts on the coastline reported seeing just the grey wash of the sea, with no sign of invasion barges, the War Cabinet and their Chiefs of Staff reappraised the situation. Winston Churchill surmised with the rest of his staff, that the air attack had two objectives. The first was to close the Port of London to ocean going shipping; the second to spread terror and despair among the London populace. Meanwhile throughout the bombing raid, Winston Churchill could not help feeling enthralled by the stimulus of danger. At one stage when hearing of some stray bombing in Whitehall, he could not help himself from inventing some excuse to return to Downing Street for some important papers.

In the short daring dash to Downing Street and back, he showed a total disregard for his own safety, as he dodged from building to building, much to the alarm of his anxious bodyguard, Walter Thompson. Soon after returning from Downing Street, he could not resist the temptation to look at the raid from the rooftops of Whitehall. Again accompanied by his bodyguard, he gazed on a sight that defied description, with flames 100ft high just two miles away, but seeming to be advancing in every direction. Seeing the destruction of his beloved London at such close quarters, had a profound effect on Churchill. Suddenly deflated, he turned to his bodyguard and murmured 'It's not the buildings burning that bothers me, it's the thought of those poor civilians. Take me downstairs Walter, I cannot bear it any longer.'

Back in the East End, the fires and bombing continued and increased in unending intensity. Many of the fire watchers and ARP wardens were overwhelmed by the scale of the fires, with most of them doing their inadequate best, while others gave up the struggle. However, the four members of the ARP Post based in Globe Road Prmary School were made of sterner stuff. It would not have entered their minds to do anything but give assistance in any way they could. As the four of them continued to snuff out the incendiaries in the Mile End Road, there suddenly came the unmistakable screaming of an approaching bomb. For a split second there was total silence, then the ground seemed to rise, followed by a massive explosion. All of them had instinctively dived low to take cover, as the explosion was followed by a rising cloud dust and the sound of breaking glass. Ted and Arthur were the first to rise, their ears ringing with the reverberation of the blast.

In the initial silence after the bomb, they could faintly hear the rustle of water from fractured pipes. As Harry and Jimmy rose unsteadily to their feet, Ted could just make out through the smoke and dust that a bomb had hit a block of flats across the road. Harry looked up at the smoke filled sky and remarked, 'Looks like Jerry is spreading it's wings, where's our gunners?' Arthur Turnbull replied, 'That's a good question, I can only assume some of those planes up there are ours.' As they moved closer they could see that the flats had lost a whole wall, with beds and furniture hanging out of the side. It was then that they heard above the din of the fire engines, the faint cries of the trapped and wounded. Turnbull was the first to react.

'Christ, there are some people in there! Let's shift this debris,' Within minutes they were joined by other wardens and firemen who had been drawn to the explosion. Ted and Arthur had clambered on to a pile of pulverized plaster and charred wood, using their torches to try and pinpoint where the voices were coming from.

Meanwhile Harry and Jimmy had gone to the rear of the building in search of the trapped victims. It was as Ted was clearing some loose bricks, that he heard a shout of alarm, followed by the dull thud of a wall collapsing. Shining his torch in the direction of the noise, he could see that the collapse had occurred in the vicinity of Harry and Jimmy. For one split second Ted's blood ran cold, before he shouted,

'Harry, are you alright?' Ted could feel his heart thumping wildly in the five seconds it took for Harry to shout back. 'I'm fine, but I think Jimmy's trapped.'

Ted felt the tangible sense of relief course through his body, before he scrambled down from the heap of rubble. When Arthur and Ted reached the scene, they could see that Jimmy had been very lucky. The collapsed wall had pinned a long beam of wood across where Jimmy lay, but the weight was still being flimsily supported by the remaining bricks. Arthur could see that any delay in freeing Jimmy could be fatal, as the slightest movement in the structure could crush him. Showing a complete disregard for the danger to himself, Arthur crawled as near as he dare, and reached out for Jimmy's hands. On Arthur's instruction, Jimmy gripped the outstretched hands as tightly as he could manage. Arthur then proceeded to slowly drag Jimmy from under the precarious beam, and mercifully away from the overhanging bricks.

Once clear, Jimmy rose groggily to his feet, and was led away by Ted and Harry. They were to spend the next four hours engrossed in grim work. From helping the firemen and ambulance staff pull people from the ruins, to administering first aid and comfort to the wounded and dying, they single mindedly steeled themselves for their mission. At one stage Harry reached into a pile of timber and bricks to grasp an outstretched hand, only to find after pulling, that he was holding a dismembered limb. When their grueling work was finally completed in the Mile End Road, they wearily made their way back to the ARP Post, carefully negotiating the fire stricken, bomb ridden streets. Back in Globe Road Primary, ArthurTurnbull ordered Ted and Harry to replenish the sand buckets, as the huge amount of incendiary bombs had exhausted their ready to hand supply. The sacks of sand were stored in a small storeroom in the basement. As Ted and Harry neared the door, they could hear the pitiful sound of someone sobbing. Curious, Ted opened the door and peered into the gloom, he could just make out what looked like a bedraggled rag doll lying limply on the floor. Ted moved gently forward before asking, 'Who is that?'

The weeping stopped and there was a short silence before someone replied, 'Have we won yet Ted?' As Ted moved further forward he recognised the familiar figure of Little Sid. He was holding a small faded photograph of his parents tightly to his chest.

The All Clear siren finally sounded at 4.30am, and in the Cabinet War Rooms there was a collective sigh of relief. Almost immediately there was a mass exodus, as staff made the most of the opportunity to get some fresh air and daylight.

Winston Churchill immediately returned to Downing Street, and after a few hours sleep, he awoke to partake of a hearty breakfast that included cold pheasant, as was his custom. After reading the documents in his dispatch boxes, he had retired to his bathroom for a long soak. His time in the bath was important to him. It gave him solitary moments to think and to plan. Languishing in the hot water, he reflected on the traumatic events of the previous day. If, as it appeared, the German's had redirected their air attacks from the military targets such as airfields to civilians in London, he felt they had made a foolish mistake. His conclusion was that by departing from the classical principles of war, the German's had given Britain much needed breathing space, and a precious opportunity to repair the badly damaged runways.

Sitting in the comfortable drawing room at Downing Street an hour later, he was conversing with two much trusted members of his 'kitchen cabinet', Brendan Bracken and Professor Frederick Lindemann. The two men provided an interesting contrast. Bracken with his unruly red hair and thick glasses, sitting next to the immaculately dressed Professor. Both men, however, were of the highest intelligence, and perfectly reflected Churchill's own characteristics of dynamism and eccentricity. Professor Lindemann was Churchill's scientific adviser, and he was giving a progress report on radar enhancement, and ways of deflecting the innovative beams that guided the German bombers to their targets. Totally absorbed in their 'Wizard War' discussion, they were suddenly interrupted by the War Cabinet secretary Edward Bridges. He politely informed Churchill that the Cabinet members were assembled in the cabinet room. Completely fascinated by his conversation on the scientific advancements of warfare, Churchill had lost all track of time. Apologising for his lateness, Churchill took his place around the cabinet table, and lit his fourth Havana of the day. The Secretary of State for War, Anthony Eden was the first to speak.

'Before we proceed, I would just like to inform you that I have some figures before me relating to last night's bombing.' Churchill nodded his assent. Eden went on. 'There were 430 civilian deaths, and 16,000 seriously injured.' Churchill looked grim as he asked, 'And the extent of the infrastructure damage?' Arthur Greenwood read from a piece of paper. 'Heavy damage to housing, particularly in the Silvertown area, and much fracturing of water, gas and sewage mains.' He paused before adding, 'in some cases drinking water is contaminated. The emergency services are performing miracles dousing the remaining fires, and endeavoring to restore vital utilities.' Churchill looked strained as he asked, 'and the homeless?'

Greenwood paused briefly before answering, 'The Salvation Army and the Women's Voluntary Service are doing their best to provide shelters for these unfortunate people.' The faces around the table looked glum, as Churchill then enquired about the conditions in the Port of London. This time it was the turn of Clement Atlee to reveal the unpleasant detail.

'In the dock before yesterday there had been 1.5 million tons of softwood, latest reports suggest four fifth's have been destroyed. The Port of London is now closed, and all shipping and vessels are being rerouted to working ports around our coasts.' Winston Churchill's expression was one of pugnacious belligerence as he began his address.

'Yesterday the German bombers had the luxury of minimal resistance in terms of anti-aircraft fire, if, as I expect, General Pile can concentrate our firepower in London over the next 24 hours, it will be a luxury they will never enjoy again. Indeed, I have just come from a conversation with Professor Lindemann about our progress as regards air defence, the electronic advancements that will soon be in use gives me great cause for optimism. Pray gentlemen, three or four times in these months the enemy has abandoned a method of attack. The early operations sought to engage our air forces in battle over the Channel and the south coast, next the struggle was continued over Kent and Sussex, mainly to destroy our airfield installations. Now it would appear that London has become the supreme target. Their object is twofold; to break the spirit of the Londoner, and to render the world's largest city uninhabitable. That they will not succeed in this objective I am certain. For by departing from the hitherto accepted dictates of humanity in the rules of war, I feel they have made a grave tactical error.' After further discussions about the likelihood of air attacks that evening, the cabinet members gradually made their exits, leaving Churchill alone with secretary Edward Bridges. Turning to Bridges, he said, 'I must visit the East End. Have I got time to get down there this morning?' Bridges, looking slightly perturbed, answered 'Not really, you have some meetings after lunch with the chiefs of staff and,' Churchill brusquely interrupted him at this point.

'Edward, I will forgo my lunch today, as it is my moral duty to visit those poor people.' Within 20 minutes, Churchill's specially armoured

Black Humber Pullman, was speeding eastwards along the embankment. Accompanying Churchill was his trusted bodyguard and friend Walter Thompson, plus his regular chauffeur Joseph Bullock. Churchill was almost never punctual in his appointments, and Bullock had soon learned to save time by shooting red lights and steering the wrong side of traffic islands. Within minutes they were among the shattered ruins of the mean houses that surrounded the docks.

It was only when he had heard the continuous wail of the All Clear siren, that Ted suddenly realised just how drained he felt, following the horrific events of the evening. Barely able to stand as he put down two buckets of sand, he could hear Arthur telling Jimmy and Harry to get home and have some shut eye. As Ted joined them and was about to go home, Arthur approached and said 'Well, that was a night that sorted the men from the boys,' he paused briefly before adding 'and I am proud to say that you three passed the test.'

After the momentary awkward silence that followed, Ted heard himself saying, 'You did not do too bad yourself.' In the following brief moment when they caught each other's glance, there was something approaching mutual respect. Ted realised that though there were elements of Arthur's character that he would never warm too, he found it easy to admire his obvious qualities of patriotism and courage. As they departed they were left with the rare sight of Arthur grinning, as he reminded them to be ready for a repeat performance that evening.

On reaching Ted's house in Three Colts Lane. Elsie, who had been waiting anxiously for Ted's return, told Harry that Joyce and the girls had gone home. Scarcely able to put one foot in front of the other, an exhausted Harry tottered on up the Lane to his own bed. Ted meanwhile had barely enough strength to climb the stairs, before collapsing into welcome oblivion. Several hours later Ted was awakened by the sound of someone knocking on the front door. Elsie stirred in her sleep next to him, and grunted 'What's the time?' Ted sat up and looked at his watch. 'Blimey it's 11 o'clock.' He eased out of the bed, and went to the window that looked out onto the Lane. Pulling the curtains, his eyes had difficulty adjusting to the brightness of the day. Lifting the sash window, Ted looked down to see Little Sid looking up at him. In their exhaustion at the end of the raid, they had completely forgotten that Sid was still cowering in the school basement store room when the All Clear had sounded. Sid had obviously finally felt it was safe enough for him to leave the dark confines of his refuge, 'Are you going to the market today?' Sid enquired. Making a conscious effort to be polite, Ted answered, 'Not today Sid, might see you later,' before firmly closing the window.

An hour later Ted was feeling much restored, after some tea and toast, and a warm bath. After the chaos and bedlam of the night before, Ted appreciated getting back to some kind of normality, even though he knew it could only be temporary. As Ted tended to his garden allotment, he could here Harry's eldest daughter Violet in the kitchen. She was telling Rita about a large bomb that had exploded near her home in Stepney Green, causing massive damage. Meanwhile Old Jack Walker had taken up his usual position on the garden fence.

'Have you heard the rumours Ted?' Ted looked up from his tomatoes and answered, 'No Jack, but I'm sure you're going to tell me.'

Old Jack needed little encouragement. 'The Germans tried to invade last night at Sandwich Bay but failed, they reckon the waters are black with German dead.' Not totally happy with Ted's muted reaction to this scoop, Jack went on, 'they reckon that the Germans have completed a cross-channel tunnel to Dover, and are launching bombs at this moment.' Ted did his best to look more intrigued, as he carried on with his allotment maintenance. It was at this point that they suddenly heard the excited voice of Harry, as he made his way through the house. Harry, looking flushed and animated, was followed by Elsie, Rita and Violet as he entered the garden. Barely able to contain himself, Harry shouted, 'You won't Adam and Eve it! Guess whose in the Whitechapel Road?' Before anyone could reply, Harry blurted out the answer, 'only old Winnie!' Within seconds they were joining the rest of the crowd scampering down the Cambridge Heath Road, as the word spread of Churchill's presence.

Winston Churchill had been profoundly affected by his visit to Silvertown. Typically, the destruction had been visited upon the civilian population with ruthless Germanic efficiency.

At one stage Churchill had vacated the car to inspect an area that had been stricken by a landmine. It had completely destroyed a row of 30 small three storey houses, and the strong smell of gas was prevalent everywhere. Amazingly among the ruins, small Union Jack flags had been planted at regular intervals. On the edge of an enormous crater, a young family stood by an upturned Anderson shelter. Churchill was amazed and deeply touched, when upon seeing him, they grinned and waved cheerily. As the black Humber entered the Whitechapel Road on it's return journey, the car was recognised, and people came running from all quarters. Within minutes they were surrounded on all sides by cheering and affectionate crowds.

As the Humber ground slowly to a halt, Churchill lit a cigar and again vacated the car, much to the agitation of Walter Thompson. As Churchill strode among the cheering backslapping crowds, there were cries of 'Are we downhearted?' To which there was a booming response from the masses 'No-o-o-o!' Ted and Harry reached the Whitechapel Road some way ahead of Elsie, Rita and Violet. Their eyes fixed on Winston Churchill almost immediately, and the effect left them spellbound. There was their leader striding among the ruins, looking exactly as they would have imagined – bowtie, gold knobbed cane, and smoking a cigar. As Churchill came towards them, Harry was unable to resist a comment.

'Are we going to give it to 'em back?' Churchill stopped and looked Harry straight in the eye. His look was tough, bulldogged, and piercing. In a clear resonant voice he answered, 'I vow to you now sir, that they will get it back tenfold'. This statement was greeted with an enormous cheer, as Churchill and his bodyguard headed back in the direction of their car.

As Ted stood transfixed among the ruins and destruction, he was struck by the certainty of not only Churchill, but also of the people. It seemed that the insular security inherent in an island race, had given the English an invincible sense of their own superiority. With memories of the previous night's horrors still fresh in his thoughts, and the inevitability of more peril yet to come, Ted found himself wishing from the depths of his soul that he could share their optimism. As the car drew away from the cheering crowds, Churchill was visibly moved, his eyes moist with pride and admiration. Still looking out of the window he remarked, 'Do you know gentlemen, the British are a truly remarkable people.' His chaffeur Joseph Bullock replied over his shoulder, 'It is down to you Mr Churchill, you are a great source of comfort and inspiration to them'. Churchill replied immediately 'Nonsense Joe, these people have the heart of a lion. I merely provide them with the roar'.

Ted and Harry stood and watched as the rear of the Humber gradually disappeared into the distance, cruising it's way westward along the Whitechapel Road.

ND - #0327 - 270225 - C0 - 234/156/10 - PB - 9781780910567 - Matt Lamination